CHARLES BERLITZ

BOOK
ON
UNEXPLAINED
DISAPPEARANCES

"FRANKLY, IT'S SPELLBINDING!"*

Charles Berlitz

The Bermuda Triangle

With the collaboration of
J. Manson Valentine

 AVON
PUBLISHERS OF BARD, CAMELOT, DISCUS, EQUINOX AND FLARE BOOKS

AVON BOOKS
A division of
The Hearst Corporation
959 Eighth Avenue
New York, New York 10019
Copyright © 1974 by Charles Berlitz
Published by arrangement with Doubleday & Company, Inc.

Library of Congress Catalog Card Number: 74-3691

ISBN: 0-380-00465-8

First Avon Printing, September, 1975

AVON TRADEMARK REG. U.S. PAT. OFF. AND
FOREIGN COUNTRIES, REGISTERED TRADEMARK—
MARCA REGISTRADA, HECHO EN CHICAGO, U.S.A.

Printed in the U.S.A.

To the sea and its mysteries—
whose solution may tell us more about ourselves . . .

Contents

The Bermuda Triangle

1

The Bermuda Triangle:
A Mystery of the Air and Sea

THERE IS A SECTION OF THE WESTERN ATLANTIC, off the southeast coast of the United States, forming what has been termed a triangle, extending from Bermuda in the north to southern Florida, and then east to a point through the Bahamas past Puerto Rico to about 40° west longitude and then back again to Bermuda. This area occupies a disturbing and almost unbelievable place in the world's catalogue of unexplained mysteries. This is usually referred to as the Bermuda Triangle, where more than 100 planes and ships have literally vanished into thin air, most of them since 1945, and where more than 1,000 lives have been lost in the past twenty-six years, without a single body or even a piece of wreckage from the vanishing planes or ships having been found. Disappearances continue to occur with apparently increasing frequency, in spite of the fact that the seaways and airways are today more traveled, searches are more thorough, and records are more carefully kept.

Many of the planes concerned have vanished while in normal radio contact with their base or terminal destination until the very moment of their disappearance, while others have radioed the most extraordinary messages, implying that they could not get their instruments to function, that their compasses were spinning, that the sky had turned yellow and hazy (on a clear day), and that the ocean (which was calm nearby) "didn't look right" without further clarification of what was wrong.

One group of five planes, a flight of Navy TBM Avengers, on a mission from the Fort Lauderdale Naval Air Station, on December 5, 1945, were the object, along with the Martin Mariner sent to rescue them and which also disappeared, of one of the most intensive ground-sea rescue operations ever conducted, although no life rafts, oil slicks, or wreckage was ever located. Other aircraft, including passenger planes, have vanished while receiving landing instructions, almost as if, as has been mentioned in Naval Board of Inquiry procedures, they had flown through a hole in the sky. Large and small boats have disappeared without leaving wreckage, as if they and their crews had been snatched into another dimension. Large ships, such as the *Marine Sulphur Queen,* a 425-foot-long freighter, and the U.S.S. *Cyclops,* 19,000 tons with 309 people aboard, have simply vanished while other ships and boats have been found drifting within the Triangle, sometimes with an animal survivor, such as a dog or canary, who could give no indication of what had happened—although in one case a talking parrot vanished along with the crew.

Unexplained disappearances in the Bermuda Triangle have continued to the present day and no plane or ship is reported as overdue and finally classed as "search discontinued" by the Seventh Coast Guard without the expressed or unexpressed comment or feeling among the public or the searchers that there is some connection with the past and present phenomenon of the Bermuda Triangle. There seems to be a growing public awareness that something is very wrong with this area. Recent numerous reports from planes and boats which have had incredible experiences within the Triangle and *survived* are contributing toward a new folklore of the sea, although the cause of the unexplained menace to planes and ships within this area is as mysterious as ever.

The most varied and imaginative explanations have been offered and seriously considered to account for the continuing disappearances and assumed (because no bodies have been recovered) fatalities. These explanations include sudden tidal waves caused by earthquakes, fireballs which explode the planes, attacks by sea monsters, a time-space warp leading to another dimension, electromagnetic or gravitational vortices which cause planes to crash and ships to lose themselves at sea, capture and kidnaping by flying or submarine UFOs manned by entities from surviving cultures of antiquity, outer space, or the *future,* looking for specimens of currently existing earth inhabitants. One of the most striking suggestions was actually predicted by Edgar Cayce, the "sleeping prophet," a psychic and healer who died in 1944. Cayce predicted, decades before the possibility of laser beams was suspected, that the ancient Atlanteans used crystals as a power source, specifically located in the Bimini area, and presumably subsequently sunk in the Tongue of the Ocean off Andros, in the Bahamas, where many of the disappearances have taken place. In this concept, a maverick power source sunk a mile deep to the west of Andros would still be exerting its occasional pull on the compasses and electronic equipment of today's ships and planes.

In any case the explanation or solution to the mystery seems connected with the sea, itself the last and greatest mystery still confronting the inhabitants of the earth. For, although we stand on the threshold of space, somewhat wistfully contemplating the cosmos while believing that the world, now so thoroughly explored, has not more mystery for us, it is nevertheless true that about three fifths of the world's area, the abyssal depths of the sea, are about as clearly or even less known to us as the craters of the moon. We have, of course, long mapped the general contours of the sea bottom, first through mechanical soundings and more recently by sonar and exploration by submarine and bathysphere, plus deep-sea camera probes charted its surface and undersea currents and are presently prospecting for evidence of oil on the continental shelves and soon perhaps at even greater depths.

Cold war activity and increasing reliance on submarine fleets, despite the danger to submarine activity experienced by the French Navy in the Mediterranean and to the United States Navy in the Atlantic, will certainly contribute considerably, if the material is made public, to our knowledge of the sea bottom. Nevertheless, the deepest parts of the ocean may still reserve considerable surprises for us. The abyssal plain and the adjoining canyons and depths may contain unexpected fauna. The "extinct" coelacanth, a supposedly prehistoric fish with residual limbs, was discovered to be very much alive and well in the Indian Ocean in 1938. This four-legged bluefish flourished about 60,000,000 years ago. Its last fossilized specimen, before the live one was found, had been dated at 18,000,000 years B.C.

Detailed accounts from reliable observers, many of whom had nothing to gain and much to lose in making a "sea serpent" report, have sketched or described sea creatures which resemble very much in structure the Pliocene monosaurus or ichthyosaurus, apparently still alive and well in the abyssal deep. On several occasions these creatures have been observed by hundreds of witnesses as they approached beaches and harbors situated at points varying from Tasmania to Massachusetts. The Loch Ness Monster, affectionately called "Nessie" by the local Scots, and regularly although indistinctly photographed, may be a smaller version of these giant "fish lizards," as their Greek name, *Ichthyosaurus,* is translated.

Anton Brunn, the Danish oceanographer, once observed a six-foot eel-like tadpole brought up by a trawler, and also its larval form, which, if it grew to adult size in proportion, would be seventy-two feet long.

Although no actual specimen of the giant squid has been secured, there are several indications that they may be fully as large as some of the fabled "sea serpents" and, in fact, actually may be the sea serpents seen by so many observers. The size of these giant squids can be calculated by occasional skeletal remains that have been recovered and also by disk marks on the backs of whales where the suction marks of the squids' tentacles, a result of their titanic struggles in the depths,

Copy of a contemporaneous drawing of the Gloucester sea serpent, one of the best corroborated among the many "sea serpent" sightings recorded through the centuries. It was reported as being seen by so many people off Cape Ann, Massachusetts, in August 1917, that it evoked an investigation from the Boston Society of Naturalists. Representatives of the society reportedly came within 139 yards of the monster, estimated it at ninety feet long, and clocked its swimming speed at thirty miles per hour. Shortly after the visit of the naturalists it vanished from the area.

have taken away the pigment from the whales' hides while leaving the outline.

Although we are constantly learning more about life in the ocean depths, most of our observations and recovery of specimens have been haphazard, as if explorers from outer space, to draw an analogy, had dropped nets from their spacecraft in various parts of the earth and pulled up whatever they chanced to find.

Even the sea creatures which are already familiar to us present mysteries in their migrations and breeding habits: the eels from inland Europe and America which meet for breeding in the Sargasso Sea, from where only the young reach the places from which their parents set forth; the tuna which start their migration off the coast of Brazil, travel to Nova Scotia and afterward to Europe, and then some, but only some, continue to the Mediterranean; the spiny lobsters which march across the sea bottom down the continental slope and continue on down to an unknown destination on the abyssal plain.

Other mysteries include the great trenches in the oceans, curiously all having approximately the same depth—a staggering seven miles—and the living creatures that exist on the bottom under such tremendous pressure. Then there are the ocean currents, great rivers in the sea, some of them surface currents varying in depth while others flow hundreds of feet below the surface, often in other directions to the surface currents. There is the Cromwell Current in the Pacific Ocean, which some years ago rose to the surface and then subsequently reverted to its subsurface level. Almost all currents turn; those in the Northern Hemisphere clockwise, and those in the Southern Hemisphere counterclockwise. But why is the Benguela Current an exception as it flows without turning?

The winds and the waves are further mysteries: the most sudden and violent storms occur in only two places, the hurricanes of the Caribbean and the west Atlantic area and the typhoons in the South China Sea. Sometimes, however, extremely strong waves, called seiche waves, appear on an otherwise calm sea. It is believed that these waves come from underwater landslides or earthquakes not noted on the surface or foretold by weather reports.

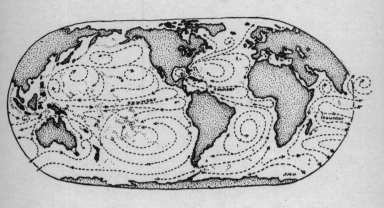

The world's main ocean currents. Note that currents in the Northern Hemisphere turn clockwise, while those in the Southern Hemisphere turn counterclockwise, a feature connected with the rotation of the earth.

The mineral wealth of the ocean is presently incalculable, and extraction and exploitation of these mineral deposits, in addition to oil, may considerably affect the financial scene of the future. The protective sea also covers treasures and vestiges of past civilizations. Many of these are evident in the shallow coastal waters of the Mediterranean and the Atlantic continental shelf, but others may lie, for example, more than a mile deep off the coast of Peru, where carved columns have been photographed lying among what may be submerged buildings indicating a tremendous downward drop of land into the ocean within the era of civilized man. Stories of sunken civilizations persist in many parts of the world's oceans—from lost Atlantis in the mid-Atlantic, the Bahamas, or the Eastern Mediterranean; the mysteries of Easter Island and other lost civilizations of the South Pacific; to the possibility of a civilization now buried under Antarctic ice, once having existed in the Antarctic before the poles shifted.

Parts of the ocean floor seem to be constantly shifting; in May 1973, part of the Bonin Trench near Japan rose 6,000 feet. The majority of the hundred thousand earthquakes which take place every year occur along the Mid-Atlantic Ridge, commonly supposed since ancient times to be the location of legendary Atlantis. Then there is the mystery of the "false bottom," frequently revealed by deep-sea soundings, which frequently report a depth much shallower than that previously recorded and then later give the first reading again. It has been assumed that this false bottom is the result of the temporary presence of banks of fish or other fauna so thick that they present a solid surface from which the sonar bounces off with resultant equivocal information. An equally baffling mystery is the curious glowing streaks of "white water" in the Gulf Stream. This is variously thought to be caused by banks of small luminescent fish, marl stirred up by fish, or radioactivity in the water. Whatever it is, it was noteworthy enough to have been commented on by Columbus five centuries ago, and it was also the last light from earth that the astronauts could see on their way to space. Finally we have the theory of drifting continents, drifting away from each other through the sea from their original position of being clustered together as a supercontinent. This theory is only now being generally accepted and may have considerable bearing on the rotation, composition, and behavior of the earth itself.

There is a difference, however, between these multiple mysteries which may eventually be solved (and which meanwhile are intriguing to contemplate) and the one posed by the Bermuda Triangle, which introduces an element of danger to the traveler. It is true, of course, that numerous planes fly over the Triangle every day, that large and small ships sail its waters, and that countless travelers visit the area every year without incident. Besides, ships and planes have been lost at sea and continue to be lost in all the world's seas and oceans for a variety of reasons (and we must remember to differentiate between "lost at sea," which suggests the finding of wreckage or some identifiable floatsam, and "disappeared," which implies none at all), but in no other area have the unexplained disappearances been so numerous, so well recorded, so sudden, and attended by such unusual circumstances, some of which push the element of coincidence to the borders of impossibility.

There are many marine or aeronautical authorities who would observe that it is perfectly natural for planes, ships, or yachts to disappear in an area where there is so much sea and air travel, subject to sudden storms and the multiple possibilities of navigational mistakes and accidents. These same authorities are likely to make the comment that the Bermuda Triangle does not exist at all, and that the very term is a misnomer, a manufactured mystery for the diversion of the curious and imaginative reader. The airlines that service the area encompassed by the Bermuda Triangle concur with this opinion with understandable enthusiasm, although there are many experienced pilots who are not so sure of its non-existence. Those who claim that the Triangle does not exist are in one sense correct, for the Bermuda Triangle of unexplained disappearances may not be a true triangle but actually more of an ellipse, or perhaps a gigantic segment of a circle with the apex near Bermuda and the curved bottom extending from lower Florida past Puerto Rico, curving south and east through the Sargasso Sea, then back again to Bermuda.

Those who have most studied the phenomenon are in general, although not specific, agreement about its location. Ivan Sanderson, who dealt with this subject in *Invisible Residents* and numerous articles, concluded that it was really an ellipse or lozenge of which there were twelve others spaced at regular intervals throughout the world, including Japan's ill-famed "Devil's Sea." John Spencer considers that the danger area follows the continental shelf, starting at a point off Virginia and going south following the American coast past Florida, continuing around the Gulf of Mexico, and including the underwater shelves of the Caribbean Islands and the periphery of Bermuda. Vincent Gaddis, author of *Invisible Horizons* and the article in *Argosy* magazine which may well have given the Bermuda Triangle its name, establishes its triangular form roughly within ". . . a line from Florida to Bermuda, another from Bermuda to Puerto Rico, and a third line back to Florida through the Bahamas"; while John Godwin in *This Baffling World* suggests that the "Hoodoo Sea" is a ". . . rough square whose limits stretch between Bermuda and the Virginia coast," with its southern boundary "formed by the Islands of Cuba, Hispañola, and Puerto Rico." Even the United States Coast Guard, which does not believe in the Bermuda Triangle, obligingly identifies its location to those requesting information about it, in the form letter—File 5720—from the Seventh Coast Guard District. It begins as follows:

> The "Bermuda or Devil's Triangle" is an imaginary area located off the southeastern Atlantic coast of the United States, which is noted for a high incidence of unexplained losses of ships, small boats, and aircraft. The apexes of the triangle are generally accepted to be Bermuda, Miami, Florida, and San Juan, Puerto Rico.

> Meteorologists frequently refer to the "Devil's Triangle" as an area bounded by lines running from Bermuda north to New York and south to the Virgin Islands, billowing fanwise west to, and encompassing, 75° WL.

A consideration of the map indicating important ship and plane disappearances on page 53 will enable the reader to draw his own conclusions as to the shape of the Bermuda Triangle, whether it is or is not a triangle at all or perhaps a small triangle within a larger one, a giant ellipse, a square, or a phenomenon paralleling the continental and island shelves.

It had long been known in maritime circles that many ships had disappeared in this area, and some of the past disappearances may have contributed to the legend of the "Sea of Lost Ships" or the "Ships' Graveyard," located in the Sargasso Sea, part of which lies within the Triangle. Records concerning disappearing ships seem to indicate disappearances with increasing frequency since the 1860s, possibly because of more detailed reporting. Disappearances began *after* the Civil War, thereby ruling out attacks by Confederate raiders. But it was some months after World War II that a startling incident occurred, suggesting that planes flying over the area could vanish from the sky for perhaps the same reason that ships had been vanishing from the sea. This was the incident that gave the Bermuda Triangle its name.

2

The Triangle of Disappearing Planes

THE BERMUDA TRIANGLE RECEIVED ITS NAME AS the result of the disappearance of six Navy planes and their crews on December 5, 1945. The first five planes that disappeared, apparently simultaneously, were on a routine training mission with a flight plan designed to follow a triangular flight pattern starting at the Naval Air Station at Fort Lauderdale, Florida, then 160 miles to the east, 40 miles to the north, and then back to their base, following a southwest course. Bermuda has given its name to what has been variously called "The Devil's Triangle," "The Triangle of Death," "The Hoodoo Sea," "The Graveyard of the Atlantic," and various other appellations, principally because it was noticed at the time that the apex of the triangular flight plan from Fort Lauderdale was in a direct line with Bermuda, and partly because Bermuda seems to be the northern boundary of both earlier and later disappearances of ships and planes in very unusual circumstances. But no incident before or since has been more remarkable than this *total* disappearance of an entire training flight, along with the giant rescue plane, a Martin Mariner with a crew of thirteen, which inexplicably vanished during rescue operations.

Flight 19 was the designation of the group of doomed planes which left their base at Fort Lauderdale on the afternoon of December 5, 1945. They were manned by five officer pilots and nine enlisted crew members, the latter detailed two to each plane but on this day short one man, who had requested removal from flying status because of a premonition and who had not been replaced. The planes were Navy Grumman TBM-3 Avenger torpedo bombers, and each carried enough fuel to enable it to cruise over a thousand miles. The temperature was sixty-five degrees, the sun was shining, there were scattered clouds and a moderate northeast wind. Pilots who had flown earlier the same day reported ideal flying weather. Flight time was calculated as two hours for this specific mission. The planes started taking off at 2 P.M. and by 2:10 P.M. they were all airborne. Lieutenant Charles Taylor, with over 2,500 hours flying time, who was in command, led the planes to Chicken Shoals, north of Bimini, where they were first to make practice runs on a target hulk. Both pilots and crews were experienced airmen and there was no reason to expect anything of an unusual nature to happen during the routine mission of Flight 19.

But something did happen, and with a vengeance. At about 3:15 P.M., after the bombing run had been accomplished and the planes had continued east, the radioman at the Fort Lauderdale Naval Air Station

Tower, who had been expecting contact from the planes regarding estimated time of arrival and landing instructions, received an unusual message from the flight leader. The record shows the following:

Flight Leader (Lieutenant Charles Taylor): Calling Tower. This is an emergency. We seem to be off course. We cannot see land. . . . Repeat . . . We cannot see land.

Tower: What is your position?

Flight Leader: We are not sure of our position. We cannot be sure just where we are. . . . We seem to be lost. . . .

Tower: Assume bearing due west.

Flight Leader: We don't know which way is west. Everything is wrong. . . . Strange . . . We can't be sure of any direction—even the ocean doesn't look as it should. . . .

At about 3:30 the senior flight instructor at Fort Lauderdale had picked up on his radio a message from someone calling Powers, one of the student flyers, requesting information about his compass readings and heard Powers say, "I don't know where we are. We must have got lost after that last turn." The senior flight instructor was able to contact the Flight 19 instructor, who told him, "Both my compasses are out. I am trying to find Fort Lauderdale. . . . I am sure I'm in the Keys, but I don't know how far down. . . ." The senior flight instructor thereupon advised him to fly north—with the sun on the portside—until he reached the Fort Lauderdale Naval Air Station. But he subsequently heard: "We have just passed over a small island. . . . No other land in sight . . ."—an indication that the instructor's plane was not over the Keys and that the entire flight, since they were unable to see land, which would normally follow a continuation of the Keys, had lost its direction.

It became increasingly difficult to hear messages from Flight 19 because of static. Apparently Flight 19 could no longer hear messages from the tower, but the tower could hear conversations between the planes. Some of these messages referred to possible fuel shortages—fuel for only seventy-five miles, references to seventy-five-mile-per-hour winds, and the unnerving observation that every gyro and magnetic compass in all the planes were off—"going crazy," as it was reported at the time—each showing a different reading. During all this time the powerful transmitter at Fort Lauderdale was unable to make any contact with the five planes, although the interplane communications were fairly audible.

By this time the personnel of the base were in an understandable uproar as news spread that Flight 19 had encountered an emergency. All kinds of suppositions concerning enemy attack (although World War II had been over for several months), or even attacks by new enemies, suggested themselves, and rescue craft were dispatched, notably a twin-engined Martin Mariner flying boat patrol plane with a crew of thirteen, from the Banana River Naval Air Station.

At 4 P.M. the tower suddenly heard that Lieutenant Taylor had unexpectedly turned over command to a senior Marine pilot, Captain Stiver. Although obscured by static and strained by tension an understandable message was received from him: "We are not sure where we are. . . . We think we must be 225 miles northeast of base. . . . We must have passed over

Florida and we must be in the Gulf of Mexico. . . ." The flight leader then apparently decided to turn 180 degrees in the hope of flying back over Florida, but as they made the turn the transmission began to get fainter, indicating that they had made a wrong turn and were flying east, away from the Florida coast over the open sea. Some reports claim that the last words heard from Flight 19 were "It looks like we are . . ." Although other listeners seem to remember more, such as: "Entering white water . . . We are completely lost. . . ."

Meanwhile the tower received a message only minutes after takeoff from Lieutenant Come, one of the officers of the Martin Mariner, dispatched to the general area where the flight was presumed to be, that there were strong winds above 6,000 feet. This, however, was the last message received from the rescue plane. Shortly after this all search units received an urgent message stating that six planes instead of five were now missing. The rescue plane, with a crew of thirteen, had disappeared as well.

No further message was ever received from the Flight 19 training mission or from the Martin Mariner that was sent to rescue them. Some time after 7 P.M., however, the Opa-Locka Naval Air Station in Miami received a faint message consisting of: "FT . . . FT . . ." which was part of the call letters of the planes of Flight 19, the instructor's plane being FT-28. But if this message was really from the "lost patrol," the time period in which it was received would indicate that the message was sent two hours *after* the planes had presumably run out of fuel.

The original air search, initiated on the day of disappearance, was suspended because of darkness, although Coast Guard vessels continued to look for survivors during the night. The next day, Thursday, an enormous search effort was started at "first light," i.e., daybreak. But in spite of one of history's most intensive searches, involving 240 planes and sixty-seven additional planes from the aircraft carrier *Solomons,* four destroyers, several submarines, eighteen Coast Guard vessels, search and rescue cutters, hundreds of private planes, yachts, and boats, and additional PBMs from the Banana River Naval Air Station and help by R.A.F. and Royal Navy units in the Bahamas, nothing was found.

A daily average of 167 flights, flying about 300 feet above the water from dawn to dusk, a minute inspection of 380,000 square miles of land and sea, including the Atlantic, Caribbean, parts of the Gulf of Mexico, and the Florida mainland and neighboring islands, with air-search time totaling 4,100 hours, revealed no life rafts, no wreckage, and no oil slicks. The beaches of Florida and the Bahamas were checked daily for a period of several weeks for identifiable flotsam from the lost planes, but without success.

All possible leads were investigated. A report that a red flare over land had been seen by a commercial plane on the day of the disappearances was first thought to be the possible explosion of the Martin Mariner, but later denied. Still later a merchant ship reported an explosion in the sky at 7:30 P.M., but if this explosion concerned the five Avengers, it would mean that they were still flying hours after their fuel reserves had been exhausted. Furthermore, to explain in this way the loss without trace of all planes would imply that they crashed together and exploded all at once after having maintained radio silence since the time contact was interrupted. It is further remarkable that no SOS messages were received from Flight 19 or the rescue mission. As far as making forced landings in the sea, the Avengers were capable of making smooth water landings and in any event could stay afloat for ninety seconds, with their crews trained to abandon ship in sixty seconds. Life rafts were available and were obtained from outside the planes. Therefore, in almost any kind of forced landing the life rafts would float and would eventually be found. During the early part of the rescue effort, some searchers noted large swells in the sea but the waves were so far apart that the planes could have landed, if necessary, in the troughs between them. The curious reference to "white water" in the last message received from Flight 19 *may* have had some connection with the thick and confusing white haze which is an occasional feature of the area. This might explain the lack of visual sighting and the report that the sun "doesn't look right," but this should not have affected the compasses and gyroscopes. In addition, there is a known radio dead spot between Florida and the Bahamas, but the planes' trouble started *before* radio contact was lost.

A Naval Board of Inquiry, after examining all available evidence and incidentally debating the court-martial of the instrument officer (who was later exonerated when it was established that all his instruments had checked out before takeoff) ended up as much in the dark as ever as to what had really happened. Part of the report states: "A radio message intercepted indicated that the planes were lost and that they were experiencing malfunctioning of their compasses." Captain W. C. Wingard, an information officer, was somewhat more direct in a subsequent press interview: ". . . Members of the Board of Inquiry were not able

to make even a good guess as to what happened."
Another Board member rather dramatically commented: "They vanished as completely as if they had
flown to Mars," thereby introducing the intriguing
elements of space travel and possible UFOs which have
since become very much a part of the Bermuda Triangle
legend. Serious investigators and oceanographers have
offered a variety of opinions as to how these and so
many other ships and planes could disappear without
trace, and how so many pilots and passengers could
completely vanish. Lieutenant Commander R. H.
Wirsching, a training officer at the Fort Lauderdale
Naval Air Base at the time of the incident, who has
considered the case for many years, thinks that the
word "disappear" is an important factor concerning the
fate of the crew of Flight 19 as no proof has ever
been adduced that they effectively perished. (A mother
of one of the lost pilots who attended the naval hearing
stated at the time that she had received the impression
that her son "was still alive somewhere in space.")
And Dr. Manson Valentine, a scientist who has watched
the area for many years from Miami, was quoted in
the Miami *News* as saying: "They are still here, but in
a different dimension of a magnetic phenomenon that
could have been set up by a UFO." A Coast Guard
officer, a member of the Board of Inquiry, expressed
himself with rather refreshing frankness as he observed
simply, "We don't know what the hell is going on out
there." And a final, more formal statement from another officer of the Board expressed the consensus of
the investigating officers: ". . . This unprecedented
peacetime loss seems to be a total mystery, the strangest
ever investigated in the annals of naval aviation."

There are often elements of incredible coincidence

connected with disasters, especially when they take place at sea (when the freighter *Stockholm* collided with the passenger ship *Andrea Doria,* a young girl who spoke only Spanish was snatched from her cabin on the *Andrea Doria* by the prow of the *Stockholm* and telescoped with part of her cabin into the bulkhead of the *Stockholm* next to the cabin of a seaman who was the only person on *his* ship who could speak Spanish), and the loss of Flight 19 was no exception to this element of coincidence.

Commander R. H. Wirshing, then a lieutenant on duty as a training officer at the Fort Lauderdale base, and from whose firsthand notes much of the above material has been coordinated, remembers that there also had been a morning training flight on the same day that was somewhat unusual. This previous flight, which, being considerably less sensational, has been generally neglected in the press reports of the disaster, also experienced compass malfunction and, instead of returning to base, landed fifty miles to the north.

A presentiment of disaster seemed to have affected at least two members of Flight 19. One was the flight instructor himself. At 1:15 P.M. he arrived late at the preflight briefing and requested of the duty officer that he be relieved from this particular assignment. His request was not accompanied by any explanation whatever; he simply stated that he did not wish to take part in the mission. As no relief was available, however, his request was denied.

A second case, that Lieutenant Wirshing personally witnessed, was the much commented on incident whereby a Marine corporal, Allan Kosnar, scheduled to fly on Flight 19, did not report to the flight line. He has been quoted in the press as saying: "I can't explain why, but for some strange reason I decided not to go on the flight that day." According to Lieutenant Wirshing, however, the corporal, a veteran of Guadalcanal, had only four months to serve before being discharged and had requested several months previously to be relieved from flight status. On the day of the flight the matter had come up again and Lieutenant Wirshing had told him to report to the flight surgeon to request his removal from flight duty. He did this and the flight subsequently took off with one member short. When the first indications of trouble with Flight 19 became evident, Lieutenant Wirshing went to the enlisted men's barracks for volunteers. The first person he met there was the recently grounded corporal, who said: "Remember you told me to see the flight surgeon? I did, and he relieved me of flight orders. That is my flight that is lost."

A report from the flight line, however, indicated that the planes had gone out with full complements, as if someone else had climbed aboard at the last minute. This caused hourly musters at the station in order to find out if anyone else was missing. When it was ascertained that no further personnel were unaccounted for, the additional mystery of the "full complement report" became just one more unsolvable element in the multiple disappearance.

Still another unusual element in the mystery of Flight 19 became public twenty-nine years after the incident when Art Ford, reporter, author, and lecturer who has followed the case since 1945, made a startling revelation over a national TV program in 1974, indicating that Lieutenant Taylor had said, over his radio, "Don't come after me. . . . they look like they are from outer space." Ford states that this original infor-

mation was given to him at the time of the happening
by a ham-radio operator but that he did not give much
credence to it, considering the difficulties of an amateur
operator receiving communications from moving aircraft and also the excitement and rumors prevalent at
the time of the incident.

But Ford, later in his investigations, received some
unusual corroboration in a transcript of the plane to
tower messages included in a subsequent report brought
on by pressure from parents of the missing personnel.
The official and formerly secret transcript, which Ford
states he was permitted to examine in part only, contained at least one phrase—"Don't come after me"—
in common with that supplied to Ford by the civilian
short-wave-radio operator and, significantly, never previously released. This final mystery, with its suggestion
of other-world interference, is echoed in more than a
few of the other disappearances.

While scores of ships and pleasure craft have disappeared in the area of the Bermuda Triangle before and
since this incident, it is noteworthy that the disasters
which jointly befell the Avengers and the Martin
Mariner were the first occasion in which planes were
affected and where there were so many efficient air-sea-
land units to conduct such an extensive and thorough,
although fruitless, search. This incident would cause
intensified search efforts in the case of plane disappearances yet to come, not only with the aim of rescu-
ing the survivors but also, after probable survival time
had run out, to find out what had happened to them.

After the incident of Flight 19, unexplained disappearances of commercial, private, and military aircraft
seemed to occur with distressing regularity in addition
to the "normal" vanishing of large and small ships

which had gone on for scores of years before. Now, however, with air-sea rescue teams, radio communications with base, more sophisticated instruments, and more highly developed search patterns, each disappearance has been investigated with considerably more thoroughness.

On July 3, 1947, a U. S. Army C-54, carrying a crew of six and flying on a routine flight from Bermuda to Morrison Army Air Field, Palm Beach, disappeared somewhere between Bermuda and Palm Beach, its last position being about 100 miles off Bermuda. An immediate, intensive air-sea search by Army, Navy, and Coast Guard units covered over 100,000 square miles of sea, although (except for some seat cushions and an oxygen bottle, *not* identified as equipment from the lost plane) no wreckage or oil slick was sighted.

As further disappearances occurred, a somewhat alarming coincidental feature was noted in that the majority of the incidents within the Triangle area seemed to take place within the peak tourist and hotel season, from November through February. Even more startling was the realization that many of the losses have occurred within a few weeks before or after Christmas. A British South American Tudor IV fourmotor passenger plane, a converted Lancaster bomber, called the *Star Tiger,* flying from the Azores to Bermuda, disappeared on January 29, 1948. It carried a crew of six and twenty-five passengers, including Sir Arthur Cunningham, a British World War II air marshal and former commander of the Second Tactical Air Force of the R.A.F. The *Star Tiger* was scheduled to land at Kindley Field, Bermuda, and at 10:30 P.M., shortly before ETA (estimated time of arrival), the pilot radioed the control tower a message including the words "Weather and performance excellent" and "Expect to arrive on schedule." The plane's position was reported as 380 miles northeast of Bermuda.

There was no further message but the *Star Tiger* never arrived. No SOS or emergency message was received or any indication that the aircraft was not functioning perfectly under optimum conditions. By midnight the *Star Tiger* was listed as overdue and by the thirtieth of January, the following day, a massive rescue-and-search operation was under way. Thirty planes and ten ships combed the area for several days without success. Some boxes and some empty oil drums were sighted northwest of Bermuda on January 31. However, if these belonged to the *Star Tiger,* it would mean that it was flying hundreds of miles off course when whatever hit it occurred and, it must be remembered, the pilot had announced nothing unusual concerning his course or the plane's operation during his last contact with the tower.

As the search continued, without success, numerous ham radio operators, along the Atlantic coast and even further inland, picked up a garbled message with the words spelled out by numbered dots—as if someone was working the sender but did not know the Morse code. The dots spelled out "Tiger." Even more weird was a report from a Coast Guard station in Newfoundland. As the taps stopped, someone had apparently sent a verbal message—simply pronouncing the following letters G-A-H-N-P. These were the call letters of the lost *Star Tiger.*

It was presumed that these various messages were hoaxes, especially considering the known erratic and lunatic behavior of certain individuals who follow and enjoy disasters. However, a disquieting similarity to the case of Flight 19 suggests itself when one remembers the faint fading message received at Miami, hours after the disappearance of the flight, which contained the flight's call letters, almost as if a final message was being sent or relayed from a far greater distance, in space or time, than would be indicated by the location where the planes had vanished.

A Court of Enquiry, under the direction of Lord Macmillan, for the investigation of the loss of the *Star Tiger* was appointed by the British Minister of Civil Aviation. Its report was published eight months after the plane's disappearance. Its findings stated that there appeared to be no grounds for supposing that the *Star Tiger* had fallen into the sea because of radio or mechanical failure, fuel exhaustion, failure to find destination, meteorological hazards, or errors of altimetry, to name a few possibilities. The design and manufacture of the Tudor IV were found to be such that there were no grounds, in the words of the report ". . . for supposing that in the design of the Tudor IV airplane or in the manufacture of the particular Tudor IV airplane, the 'Star Tiger', there were technical errors or omissions, judged against a standard of agreed good practice . . ."

The final opinion of the court could be considered equally applicable to other aircraft disappearances in the Triangle, both before and since the *Star Tiger:*

It may be truly said that no more baffling problem has ever been presented for investigation. . . . In the complete absence of any reliable evidence as to either the nature or the cause of the disaster to Star Tiger the court has not been able to do more than suggest possibilities, none of which reaches even the level of probability. Into all activities which involve the co-operation of man and machine two elements enter of very diverse character. There is the incalculable element of the human equation dependent upon imperfectly known factors; and there is the mechanical element subject to quite different laws. A breakdown may occur in either separately or in both in conjunction. Or some external cause may overwhelm both man and machine. What happened in this case will never be known.

By an extraordinary and rather disquieting coincidence occurring within twelve days before the first anniversary of the disappearance of the *Star Tiger,* her sister ship, the *Star Ariel,* carrying a crew of seven and thirteen passengers, disappeared in a flight between Bermuda and Jamaica on January 17, 1949. Her complete course was to have been from London to Santiago, Chile, and the stop at Bermuda was for the purpose of taking on enough fuel for an additional ten hours' flying time. When the *Star Ariel* left Bermuda at 7:45 A.M. the sea was calm and weather conditions were good. Her captain sent the following routine flight report back to Bermuda about fifty-five minutes after takeoff:

> This is Captain McPhee aboard the "Ariel" en route to Kingston, Jamaica, from Bermuda. We have reached cruising altitude. Fair weather. Expected time of arrival Kingston as scheduled. . . . I am changing radio frequency to pick up Kingston.

But there were no further messages from the *Star Ariel,* then or ever.

When the search for the *Star Ariel* began, there was a U. S. Navy task force on maneuvers in the same general area. Two aircraft carriers sent their planes to join Coast Guard and Air Force rescue units sent from many points along the Atlantic coast; as well as British planes sent from Bermuda and Jamaica.

Cruisers, destroyers, and the U.S. battleship *Missouri* joined the surface search along with British naval vessels and merchant ships that happened to be in the area. A radiogram to all ships at sea in the general area read as follows:

BRITISH SOUTH AMERICAN AIRWAYS FOUR ENGINED AIR-AIRCRAFT *STAR ARIEL*/GAGRE WHICH DEPARTED BERMUDA 1242 GMT 17TH JANUARY FOR JAMAICA ON TRACK TWO ONE SIX DEGREES WAS LAST HEARD FROM WHEN APPROXIMATELY 15 MILES SOUTH OF BERMUDA AT 1337 GMT 17TH JAN.
ALL VESSELS ARE REQUESTED TO REPORT TO THIS STATION THE SIGHTING OF ANY FLOATING DEBRIS IN THE NATURE OF AIRCRAFT CABIN UPHOLSTERY AND PILLOWS COLOUR BLUE, AIRCRAFT DINGHIES COLOUR YELLOW, MAE WESTS COLOUR DARK BROWN, ALL OF WHICH WOULD BE MARKED BSAA, OR ANY FLOATING CLOTHING.

Seventy-two search planes flying in close formation, at times almost "wing tip to wing tip," covered 150,000 square miles of ocean, starting in the vicinity of the last radio report and proceeding southwest toward Jamaica. They were unable to discover a single piece of evidence which could be identified with the missing plane. Reports of "a strange light" on the sea came on January 18 from both a British and a U.S. plane, but search-and-rescue units dispatched to the vicinity found nothing and the Air Force suspended search operations on January 22.

The fact that these two British passenger planes (both belonging to the same company—British South American Airways) were lost almost within a year of each other and in the same area gave rise to suspicions of sabotage, although in later days skyjacking would have immediately suggested itself. This possibility, as well as pilot and crew training, instrument functioning, and weather conditions, were investigated by a Board of Enquiry, the Brabazon Committee, which found nothing unfavorabe and no clues whatever: ". . . lack of evidence due to no wreckage having been found the cause of the accident to the 'Star Ariel' is unknown."

One theory considered at the time was that methyl bromide from the extinguishers had accidentally penetrated and circulated within the pressure system causing an explosion. This would be a possibility for a freak accident in one plane perhaps, but hardly in the many others that have vanished in the same area.

One of the reasons that the search for the *Star Ariel* had been so massive was that another passenger plane, a chartered DC-3 en route from San Juan to Miami, had, in the early morning of December 28, 1948, disappeared into the void with thirty-six passengers and crew. The fruitless search for this plane, involving over forty military planes and numerous ships, covering over 300,000 miles of ocean and coastline, had been suspended only one week before the *Star Ariel* vanished. The circumstances attending the DC-3 disappearance had been even more surprising than those of the other lost flights. As with the others, the weather was excellent and the night was clear. The plane took off at 10:30 P.M., December 27. Sometime during the night flight, the plane's captain, Robert Linquist, had observed on the radio—"What do you know? . . . We are all singing Christmas carols!" (We are reminded of the coincidental timing of the majority of the disappearing planes.)

Another message from the DC-3 was received by the Miami tower at 4:13 A.M. It was: "we are approaching the field . . . Only fifty miles out to the south . . . We can see the lights of Miami now. All's well. Will stand by for landing instructions." Nothing was ever heard from the plane again and a land-and-sea search produced no identifiable wreckage. Naturally there were no survivors or any indication as to what had happened to the passengers and crew. Since the captain had given the position of the plane as only fifty miles south of Miami, it is all the more remarkable that there was no explosion, no flare, no SOS or MAYDAY over the air. Moreover, the spot where the plane vanished was over the Florida Keys, where the clear waters, only twenty feet deep, would aid location and identification of the aircraft. This was to be one of several instances where a plane and passengers would "dematerialize" almost within the reach of a landing field, or that a ship, as we shall see in the next chapter, would vanish in sight of its home port.

Large aircraft which have disappeared since the *Star Ariel* have generally followed the same pattern— that is, normal flight procedure, then—nothing—and subsequently no trace of wreckage, oil slicks, floating debris, crew, or even suspicious concentrations of sharks.

Smaller planes also have continually disappeared. No less than nine of them vanished off the coast of Florida without trace in December 1949, a sufficient number to cause one to reflect that there was something dangerous about the area even if the pattern of disappearances had not been fairly obvious.

Planes continued to disappear during the fifties. In March 1950 a U.S. Globemaster disappeared on the northern end of the Triangle while on its way to Ireland. On February 2, 1952, a British York transport, carrying thirty-three passengers and crew, vanished on the northern edge of the Triangle while on its way to Jamaica. Some weak SOS signals were received but were almost immediately aborted.

On October 30, 1954, a U. S. Navy Constellation disappeared with forty-two passengers and crew while flying in fair weather from Patuxent River Naval Air Station, Maryland, to the Azores. More than 200 planes and many surface vessels joined in searching several hundred square miles of ocean but found nothing. As in the case of some of the other planes a scarcely identifiable SOS was at one point received shortly after the plane's disappearance.

On April 5, 1956, a B-25, converted to a civilian cargo-carrying plane, disappeared with three aboard in the vicinity of the Tongue of the Ocean, a mile-deep underwater canyon to the east of Andros Island in the Bahamas.

A U. S. Navy Martin Marlin P5M patrol seaplane vanished while on patrol in Bermuda on November 9, 1956, with a crew of ten.

A U. S. Air Force KB-50 tanker leaving from Langley Air Force Base, Virginia, on its way to the Azores, on January 8, 1962, disappeared as had the Super Constellation lost in 1954. Again, as with the Super Constellation, there was a weak radio message indicating an unspecified difficulty and then silence—and, following the pattern, no wreckage or any indication as to what had happened. In each case it must be remembered that the crews had ample lifesaving equipment in case of ditching, so that whatever happened to the planes happened unexpectedly and extremely quickly.

An incident somewhat reminiscent of the confusion recorded by the pilots of Flight 19 occurred in the case of an SOS from a private plane proceeding to Nassau, Bahamas, but flying in the vicinity of Great Abaco Island. Although the morning weather was excellent, the pilot seemed to be flying through fog and was unable to give his position or even see the islands below him, in spite of clear visibility apparent to other observers in the surrounding area. In this case the plane did not completely vanish, as a part of one wing was later found floating in the sea.

A two-plane loss that occurred on August 28, 1963, was first thought to be a disappearance but later when some wreckage was identified the mystery only deepened. Two KC-135, four-engine jet Stratotankers (the first jets lost in the Triangle), on a refueling mission out of Homestead Air Force Base, Florida, disappeared shortly after giving their position as 300 miles southwest of Bermuda. An intensive search located probable debris from the lost planes about 260 miles southwest of Bermuda, and investigators concluded that there had been a collision between the two planes. Several days later, however, more debris, thought to come from the other plane, was found 160 miles away. If they had collided in the air, despite an official Air Force statement that they were not flying close together, then something must have separated the wreckage much more quickly than the ocean currents could have done. And if they had both crashed simultaneously, perhaps as the five Avengers had, what would have caused their instruments or engines to malfunction at the same time?

In the following month, on September 22, a C-132 Cargomaster disappeared between Delaware and its destination in the Azores. The last message from the pilot indicated that all was well as he gave his position as about eighty miles off the south Jersey coast. An intensive search by planes, Coast Guard and Navy vessels continued until September 25, but found nothing that could be identified with the missing plane.

On June 5, 1965, a C-119 "Flying Boxcar" on a routine mission and carrying a crew of ten vanished while on a flight from Homestead Air Force Base to Grand Turk Island, near the Bahamas. The last call received from the C-119 gave its position as being about 100 miles from its destination, with ETA of about one hour. This was the last message, and after a search lasting five days and nights, the Coast Guard reported "Results negative"—with the familiar comment: "There are no conjectures." As in the case of Flight 19, the Avengers, and other vanishing planes, faint and unintelligible messages were picked up and soon faded out as if something was blocking radio transmission, or else that the plane was receding, as has been suggested, farther and farther into space and time. It is worthy of note that another plane flying the same route, but in the opposite direction, as the lost C-119 reported that the weather was clear and the visibility good.

Within the period 1945 to 1965, fifteen commercial airliners disappeared in this area as well as a great many military and civilian planes. The phenomenon has not given any noticeable signs of abating.

Some rather unusual circumstances accompanied the

disappearance of Carolyn Cascio, a licensed pilot, who, flying a light plane, vanished with one passenger on June 7, 1964, on a flight from Nassau to Grand Turk Island, Bahamas. When she got to the point where she calculated Grand Turk should be, she radioed that she could not find her direction and that she was circling over two unidentified islands, adding "Nothing is down there," and later "Is there any way out of this?" Strangely enough, observers on Grand Turk at that time noted that a light plane circled the island for about half an hour before disappearing. But how was it if observers could clearly see the plane, that the pilot could not see the buildings on Grand Turk?

A Chase YC-122, carrying four persons en route to Grand Bahama from Palm Beach, Florida, vanished at some point northwest of Bimini on January 11, 1967.

A recent loss on the comparatively short run from Fort Lauderdale to Freeport took place on June 1, 1973, when Reno Rigoni disappeared with his copilot, Bob Corner, in a Cessna 180. No wreckage was found anywhere in the vicinity of his indicated flight pattern in a search which included the Everglades. No distress signal was heard from their radio.

As this book goes to press, still another unusual disappearance has taken place nine hundred miles southwest of the Azores, a point marking the last sighting (February 17, 1974) of Thomas Gatch, an aspirant transatlantic balloonist. A 223,000-square-mile area was searched by United States Navy planes, but with no result. While the vastness of the ocean and inconstancy of the winds would suffice to explain the swallowing up of the balloon by the sea, the area of the disappearance is, in itself, intriguing.

While special reasons and suggestions have been

advanced in the case of each unexplained disappearance certain phrases reoccur in official reports as well as in books and articles describing the losses. The phrases include "CAT" (clear air turbulence), "wind shear," "atmospheric aberrations," "magnetic anomalies" and "electromagnetic disturbances," which would explain some of the plane losses; they would by no means explain the planes' disappearances or the many ships which have been lost in the same area.

While the Navy and Coast Guard recognize a compass variation as well as a radio dead spot within a section of the area, the official policy is still clearly expressed in the words of Captain S. W. Humphrey:

> It is not felt that an atmospheric aberration exists in this area nor that one has existed in the past. Fleet aircraft and patrol flights are conducted regularly in this same area without incident.

Nevertheless, the incidence of disappearances in the lower section of the Bermuda Triangle, especially the Bahamas, the Florida east coast, and the Florida Keys, has been well described by the late Ivan Sanderson, who investigated this area as well as numerous other areas of ship and plane disappearances over a period of many years:

> The number of disappearances is out of all proportion to such recorded losses anywhere else.

A pertinent observation is made by Dale Titler in his *Wings of Mystery* when he considers that by now "a considerable fleet of planes" has disappeared without trace within this small area.

All these planes were flown by experienced airmen and directed . . . by trained navigators. All carried radio and survival equipment and all disappeared in good weather.

He adds the intriguing observation that "almost all of the planes disappeared in the daytime."

Robert Burgess, another researcher and writer about phenomena of the seas, concludes in his book *Sinkings, Salvages, and Shipwrecks:*

There is reason to believe that a factor far greater than chance may be involved in these mysterious accidents.

He adds that whatever it is called, whether "an atmospheric aberration or something else, it strikes without warning frequently enough to be alarming."

As we have mentioned before, there is considerable doubt as to the boundaries of the Bermuda Triangle, as well as whether it exists at all. We have heard it described as an actual triangle, of which the northern apex is Bermuda, a great lozenge-shaped area in the western part of the North Atlantic, an area following the continental shelf of the southern United States and the Gulf of Mexico and the Antilles, or an elastic danger area extending from the Bahamas to Florida, and through Florida to the Gulf of Mexico. Whatever its exact shape, this area has given rise to an entire folklore of disappearance, whether the object is a plane, ship, yacht, sailboat, submarine, or vanishing personnel from abandoned ships. The attribution of mysterious powers to the Bermuda Triangle has become so widespread that any disappearance or mysterious accident elicits comments on, and review of, many of the other unsolved mysteries.

Comment on TV or radio usually brings forth questions from understandably concerned listeners who have been considering visiting the area by plane. Such nervous inquiries are usually answered with the assurance that there is no danger to such travel inasmuch as innumerable crossings of the Triangle have been and are being made without incident. Travel agents are sometimes hesitantly asked by passengers en route to points beyond the Triangle, "Do you fly through the Bermuda Triangle?"—a question fairly easy to answer in the negative since the Triangle's boundaries are somewhat fluid. On one recorded occasion an excuse was given to a restless passenger explaining the plane's delay: "We had to fly around the Bermuda Triangle."

A further reassurance is the fact that today's aircraft have many more safety devices than some of those that have disappeared in the past. Some of these devices were not in use at the time of some of the more striking incidents. These included transistors, decca hifix, loran (which was, however, in use on the *Star Ariel*), and the fact that even small planes now use "omni," a radio-directed homing system which enables planes to find their way back to base through the thickest clouds.

Nevertheless, despite all modern improvements, odd incidents and losses continue to occur within the Triangle and adjacent coastal lands. Within the past year, several planes mysteriously disintegrated over land within a short distance of the Miami airport, including Eastern Airlines Flight 401 (a Lockheed L-1011), with a loss of over 100 passengers and crew on December 29, 1972. Examination of the conditions of the loss of

Flight 401 may shed some light on the many flights that have disappeared suddenly over water. Dr. Manson Valentine observes:

Analyzing all available data, it is apparent that in the last *seven or eight seconds* of flight the plane descended at such a rapid rate that neither flight control at Miami nor the pilots had time to check it out; all altimeters were working so that the pilots would, under normal circumstances, have had ample correctional time: so fast was this descent (not alluded to anywhere in reports as being unusual) that Miami control had only one sweep of the radar— 40 seconds in all—to notice it; on the *second* sweep the plane had descended from 900 feet (where it was first recognized as out of the 2,000 feet prescribed path) to *less than 300 feet*. Probably it had already crashed.

This fall rate cannot be accounted for by loss of auto-pilot, stall characteristics, pilot inexperience, or even the half-power position of throttles. There *must* have been an atmospheric reason, quite probably magnetic anomaly of some sort.

When planes and boats mysteriously disappear, or in the case of a plane, disintegrate, in this area, an increasing number of people feel a lingering doubt as to whether they have been lost "normally"—that is, through unusual weather conditions, pilot fatigue or error, control faults, structural or engine failure, etc., or whether the force that often seems to snatch planes out of the sky, and ships from the surface of the sea, is still in operation. John Godwin (*This Baffling World*), in commenting on public acceptance of such a possibility, notes that American and British authorities have never officially proclaimed the Triangle area to be "a danger zone" and adds: "But privately both marine and aviation experts have confessed that they may be facing a phenomenon of environment rather than a chain of technical mishaps." He observes that whatever is happening may be as unknown to people of the present day as "the power of radium was to alchemists of the XV century." He further points out that, "although one cannot be sure that there is a connection between the vanishing ships and planes . . . all these craft were crowded into the same narrow geographical confines."

Long before the aircraft incidents of the 1940s and thereafter, the area of the sea encompassed in the Bermuda Triangle, including Cape Hatteras, the coasts of the Carolinas, and the Florida Strait, had often been referred to as the "Ships' Graveyard," the sinkings usually being caused by heavy seas and sudden storms. The Sargasso Sea is also referred to as the "Ships' Graveyard" or the "Sea of Lost Ships" for an opposite reason: that ships have been lost there not from storms but from calms. Within this general area certain mysterious disappearances of large ships without the sending of SOS signals or the subsequent findings of flotsam or bodies had already been noted through the years, but it was not until the mass plane disappearances of 1945 and thereafter and the sudden disappearances of large and small boats that researchers began to consider the recurrent pattern of disappearances. A headline in the Manchester *Guardian,* appearing at the time of the Flight 19 disappearance, is typical of this reaction. It reads: "SARGASSO GRAVEYARD NOW CLAIMS PLANES AS WELL AS SHIPS."

The disappearing planes brought the Bermuda Triangle worldwide attention. But for more than 170

years, and perhaps before records were available, ships
large and small have been disappearing with their crews
(and crews have also been vanishing from their ships)
within the Bermuda Triangle. Some of the incidents
connected with these marine disasters possess features
strongly reminiscent of the mysterious losses by air
while others present unusual and surprising peculiarities.

Major aircraft disappearances in Bermuda Triangle area
(numbers in circles)

1. December 5, 1945: five TBM Navy Avenger
   bombers on training flight from Fort Lauderdale,
   Florida; total crew of fourteen; two-hour normal
   flight; lost approximately 225 miles northeast of
   base.
2. December 5, 1945: PBM Martin bomber; dispatched with crew of thirteen to assist the TBM
   patrol; twenty minutes later radio contact lost and
   plane disappeared.
3. 1947: Superfort (U. S. Army C-54) disappeared
   100 miles off Bermuda.
4. January 29, 1948: *Star Tiger,* four-engine Tudor
   IV; lost radio contact after last contact 380 miles
   northeast of Bermuda; plane lost with thirty-one
   passengers and crew.

OPPOSITE:
*Chart of major disappearances of planes and ships in
the Bermuda Triangle with indication of approximate
location at time of disappearances. Plane disappearances are indicated by numbers within circles, and ship
disappearances by numbers within triangles. Refer to
page above and following pages for key to numbers.*

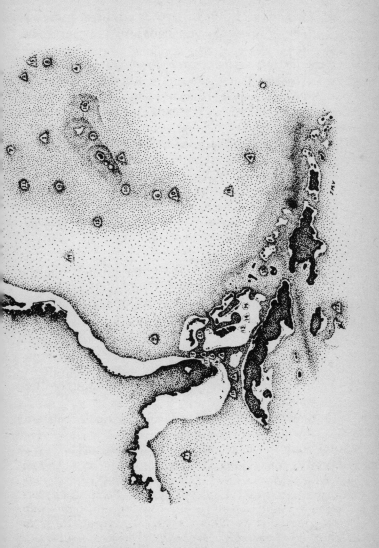

5. December 28, 1948: DC-3, private charter. San Juan, P.R., to Miami; thirty-two passengers plus crew.

6. January 17, 1949: *Star Ariel,* sister ship of *Star Tiger;* London to Santiago, Chile, via Bermuda and Jamaica; radio communication lost 380 miles south-southwest of Bermuda on course to Kingston.

7. March 1950: Globemaster (American); disappeared on northern edge of Triangle en route to Ireland..

8. February 2, 1952: York Transport (British); disappeared north of Triangle en route to Jamaica; thirty-three aboard.

9. October 30, 1954: Super Constellation (Navy); vanished north of the Triangle with forty-two aboard.

10. November 9, 1956: Navy Martin patrol seaplane P5M; disappeared with crew of ten near Bermuda.

11. January 8, 1962: Air Force tanker KB-50; Langley Field, Virginia, to Azores.

12. August 28, 1963: two new Air Force KC-135 four-engine Stratotankers; Homestead Air Force Base, Florida, to classified refueling range in Atlantic; disappeared 300 miles southwest of Bermuda.

13. June 5, 1965: C-119 Flying Boxcar; ten aboard; lost in the southeast Bahamas.

14. April 5, 1956: B-25 converted to civilian cargo plane; lost southeast of Tongue of the Ocean; three aboard.

15. January 11, 1967: Chase YC-122, converted to cargo; four aboard; lost in the Gulf Stream between Palm Beach and Grand Bahama.

16. September 22, 1963: C-132 Cargomaster vanished en route to Azores.

Major ships disappeared or found derelict in Triangle area
(*numbers in triangles*)

1. 1840: *Rosalie,* a large French vessel; found on course to Havana from Europe, in Triangle area, with sails set, cargo intact, all hands missing.

2. January 1880: British frigate *Atalanta;* left Bermuda for England with 290 aboard; vanished presumably not far from Bermuda.

3. October 1902: German bark *Freya;* found soon after leaving Manzanillo, Cuba, listing badly, partly dismasted, anchor dangling; calendar in captain's cabin read October 4—day after sailing.

4. March 4, 1918: U. S. Navy supply ship U.S.S. *Cylcops,* 500 feet, 19,000 tons displacement; sailed March 4 from Barbados to Norfolk with 309 aboard; no bad weather; no radio messages; no wreckage ever found.

5. 1925: S.S. *Cotopaxi;* vanished en route from Charleston to Havana.

6. April 1932: two masted *John and Mary;* New York registry; found floating but abandoned fifty miles south of Bermuda; sails furled, hull freshly painted.

7. February 1940: Yacht *Gloria Colite* from St. Vincent, B.W.I.; found abandoned; everything in order; 200 miles south of Mobile, Alabama.

8. October 22, 1944: Cuban freighter *Rubicon;* found by Coast Guard in Gulf Stream off Florida coast; deserted, except for a dog.

9. June 1950: S.S. *Sandra,* 350-foot freighter; sailed

from Savannah, Georgia, bound for Puerto Cabello,
Venezuela; cargo 300 tons of insecticide; passed
St. Augustine, Florida, then disappeared without
leaving a trace.

10. September 1955: Yacht *Connemara IV;* mysteriously abandoned 400 miles southwest of Bermuda.

11. February 2, 1963: *Marine Sulphur Queen,* 425-foot freighter; vanished without message, clues, or debris; en route to Norfolk, Virginia, from Beaumont, Texas, with all hands; last heard from near Dry Tortugas.

12. July 1, 1963: *Sno' Boy,* sixty-three-foot fishing boat; forty aboard; sailed from Kingston, Jamaica, to Northeast Cay, eighty miles south; disappeared with all hands.

13. 1924: *Raifuku Maru,* Japanese freighter; radioed for help between Bahamas and Cuba, then disappeared.

14. 1931: *Stavenger,* freighter with crew of forty-three; last heard from near Cat Island, Bahamas.

15. March 1938: *Anglo-Australian,* freighter with crew of thirty-nine; last message received west of Azores: "All well."

16. December 1967: *Revonoc,* all-weather forty-six-foot racing yacht; disappeared within sight of land.

17. December 24, 1967: *Witchcraft,* cabin cruiser; passenger and owner disappeared while craft was at harbor buoy one mile from Miami.

18. April 1970: *Milton Iatrides,* freighter en route from New Orleans to Capetown.

19. March 1973: *Anita,* 20,000-ton freighter with crew of thirty-two, sailing from Newport News to Germany.

3

The Sea of Lost Ships

SHIP DISAPPEARANCES WITHIN THE TRIANGLE HAVE principally occurred within the region of the western Atlantic Ocean called the Sargasso Sea, a so-called largely immobile sea named after the seaweed *Sargassum*. If anything were needed to intensify the mystery of the Triangle, such an element is provided by the Sargasso Sea, itself a mystery ever since the first Spanish and Portuguese seamen encountered it five hundred years ago. And, if we include what now seem to have been probable penetrations and crossings of it by Phoenician and Carthaginian oceangoing sailors, it has been an observed mystery for thousands of years.

The Sargasso Sea is a huge area of the western North Atlantic characterized þy the presence of a kind of floating seaweed *Sargassum,* which, lazily floating either separately or in large masses, marks the boundaries of this sea within an ocean. When Columbus on

his first voyage observed so much seaweed he mistaken-
ly deduced that land was near and was greatly encouraged by it, a sentiment not wholeheartedly shared
by his crew.

This seaweed sea is bounded on the north by the
Gulf Stream as it moves first northeast and then east
and on the west and south by the returning Gulf Stream
and the North Equatorial Current. Although somewhat
amorphous, it extends from about 37° north latitude
to about 27° south latitude and from 75° west to 40°
west. Under the deep waters of the Sargasso Sea lie the
Hatteras and Nares Abyssal plains, the precipitous
Bermuda Rise, numerous mysterious seamounts (underwater mountains rising toward the surface but termi-
nating in flat tops as if they had once been islands), and
at its eastern limits, part of the North Atlantic Ridge,
a tremendous north–south underwater mountain chain
in the middle of the Atlantic Ocean whose highest crests
break through the surface of the sea to form the Azores
Islands. In other words, a stagnant sea almost devoid
of currents except on its borders, extends from about
200 miles north of the Greater Antilles up the Florida
and Atlantic coasts at a general distance of about 200
miles from land to the vicinity of Cape Hatteras and
then out in the Atlantic in the direction of the Iberian
Peninsula and Africa up to the North Atlantic Ridge
and back again to the Americas.

The Sargasso Sea is characterized not only by its
omnipresent seaweed but by its deadly calms, a fact that
may have started the picturesque but unnerving legend
of "Sea of Lost Ships," the "Graveyard of Lost Ships,"
and the "Sea of Fear." This sailors' legend told of a
great Atlantic surface graveyard containing ships from
all the ages of seafaring man, caught and immobilized

in fields of seaweed, slowly decaying but still manned by skeleton crews, or rather crews of skeletons, comprised by the unfortunates who could not escape and shared the doom of their ships. In this area of death were to be found tramp steamers, yachts, whalers, clippers, packets, brigantines, pirate vessels, and, to make the story better, Spanish treasure galleons. In enthusiastic retelling of the stories, the tellers included other ships that should certainly have rotted away and disappeared by the time of the telling, such as the dragon ships of the Vikings with skeletons still at their oars, Arab sailing galleys, Roman triremes with their great banks of oars, Phoenician trading ships with silver anchors, and even the great ships of lost Atlantis, their bows covered with fitted gold plate—all doomed to rot for centuries in a motionless sea.

The first legends about the Sargasso Sea may stem from the Phoenicians and Carthaginians who possibly crossed it thousands of years ago and made landfalls in the Americas, as indicated by the many Phoenician stone inscriptions in Brazil, and some in the United States, caches of Phoenician coins found first in the Azores, Carthaginian coins later found in Venezuela and the southeast coast of the United States as well as ancient pictorial representations of what appear to be Semitic visitors in Mexico. The following report from the Carthaginian admiral Himilco, made in 500 B.C., strikes a familiar if somewhat sensational chord in reference to the seaweed fields and lack of winds in the Sargasso Sea:

> . . . No breeze drives the ship, so dead is the sluggish wind of this idle sea. . . . there is much seaweed among the waves, it holds back the ship like bushes.

. . . the sea has no great depth, the surface of the
earth is barely covered by a little water. . . . the
monsters of the sea move continuously to and fro
and fierce monsters swim among the sluggish and
slowly creeping ships. . . .

Admiral Himilco may be pardoned a certain understandable exaggeration across the vault of time, and
besides the Phoenico-Carthaginian ocean travelers were
most anxious to discourage other travelers of the time
from sailing past the Pillars of Hercules (Gibraltar) at
the entrance to the Mediterranean into the ocean sea
beyond. This was primarily to keep to themselves the
profitable trade they had with cultures of the Atlantic
coasts of Europe and Africa and perhaps even farther
afield. The Carthaginians even had a mandatory death
sentence for their sea captains who betrayed their routes
or even their presence on the Atlantic, a factor which
explains the Carthaginian penchant for sinking *all*
strange ships near or past Gibraltar or, when not strong
enough to do so, to escape notice, scuttling their own
craft if necessary.

Other ancient writers have embroidered on these
early reports and have commented on the shoals and
shallows in the Atlantic left by the subsidence of the
lost continent of Atlantis as well as the seaweed which
enmeshed the oars and stopped the galleys. Like most
legends the "Sea of Lost Ships" could have some
basis in reality, although embroidered with fantasy
and dreams. The Australian Alan Villiers, a lifelong
sailor who, when crossing the Sargasso Sea on a sailing
ship, actually observed an abandoned ship among the
seaweed, points out (*Wild Ocean,* 1957) that, if a ship
were becalmed long enough to use up her stores, she

would ". . . eventually grow grass and barnacles until she became virtually unable to sail . . ." And that tropical borer worms would bore into the sides of the vessel until ". . . a rotted and putrid mess, manned by skeletons . . . slipped below the heated surface of the calm sea."

Among the many derelicts that have been sighted in the Sargasso Sea within modern times are some that, although not enmeshed in seaweed, have been becalmed and abandoned through lack of wind.

Even the name of the Horse Latitudes, which traverse the Sargasso Sea, is an indication of the stagnant calm, for when the Spanish galleons were becalmed and the drinking water began to run low, the Spaniards were reluctantly forced to kill and jettison their warhorses in order to conserve water.

Modern motor ships no longer run the risk of being becalmed—a fact that makes the numerous ship disappearances there even more mysterious. Of course *all* ship losses are mysterious inasmuch as relatively few captains set out to lose their ships. When the fate of a ship is established or even assumed, the mystery ceases. This has not been the case with the many ships that have disappeared in the Sargasso Sea.

In the early recorded days of disappearances in the Sargasso Sea and its bordering Gulf Stream area, many losses were set down to weather or pirates, although Spanish records were surprisingly well kept, no doubt because of the value of the cargoes borne by the galleons of the yearly treasure fleets to Spain. These ships, coming from Mexico, Panama, and what is now Colombia, made a rendezvous at Havana and sailed up the Keys and the Florida Strait, where many of them foundered in hurricanes and deposited their treasures

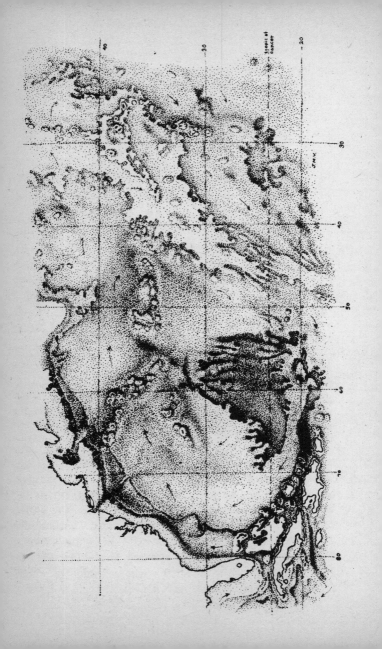

on the sea bottom for the benefit of subsequent generations of divers. Others were sunk without trace by privateers or ordinary pirates.

Long after piracy at sea ceased to be a profitable way of life, however, ships continued to disappear in this area even when the weather was good and, as would be increasingly common in later years, without depositing any wreckage or bodies along the shores and islands of the western Atlantic.

Many of these recorded disappearances concern ships of the United States and other navies, starting with the U.S.S. *Insurgent* in August 1800 with 340 men on board up to the disaster from unknown causes which overtook the submarine *Scorpion* with a crew of ninety-nine in May 1968. The *Scorpion,* however, was not a "disappearance" since it was finally located at a depth of two miles underwater at about 460 miles southeast of the Azores.

OPPOSITE:

Area occupied by the Sargasso Sea in the western North Atlantic. Arrows indicate direction of the Gulf Stream and the North Equatorial Current, which form the approximate boundaries of this seaweed-bearing and seemingly stagnant sea within the ocean, characterized by deadly calm. Depth on the chart is shown by the progressively darker areas except for small islands, such as Bermuda and the Azores, shown in solid black. Raised areas, especially between 30° and 40° north latitude, show the mysterious seamounts, underwater mountains with flat tops, suggesting that they were once islands. The shallow areas around the Azores and the Bahamas are also an indication of these islands having been of much greater size before the melting of the last glaciation raised the water level of the oceans.

Other unexplained disappearances of naval craft in this area have included the following:

The U.S.S. *Pickering* disappeared on August 20, 1800, with a crew of ninety, en route to Guadeloupe in the West Indies from New Castle, Delaware.

The U.S.S. *Wasp,* October 9, 1814, sailing in the Caribbean with a crew of 140.

The U.S.S. *Wild Cat,* October 28, 1824, en route from Cuba to Thompson's Island with a crew of fourteen.

H.M.S. *Atalanta,* January 1880, en route from Bermuda to England with total complement of 290, mostly naval cadets aboard for training. The disappearance of the *Atalanta* was the occasion for a long sea search by the British Navy. Six ships from the Channel Fleet were detailed to advance in a line separated one from another by several miles over the area in which the *Atalanta* was presumed lost. This wide search was to be repeated many times in the future when planes would fly in massive search patterns over the area—almost wing tip to wing tip. The search for the *Atalanta* continued until early May without success.

U.S.S. *Cyclops,* March 4, 1918, en route from Barbados to Norfolk, Virginia, with 309 naval personnel aboard. Among the disappearances suffered by the Navy the *Cyclops* is the best known and also the most unusual considering land-sea and ship-to-ship communications at the time of World War I as well as because of additional items of coincidence. Since the First World War was still raging, it was first thought that the *Cyclops* (a collier, or coal-supply ship, and a sister ship to the U.S.S. *Langley,* which was later converted to a U.S. aircraft carrier) had either struck a mine, encountered a German submarine or surface raider, or suffered a mutiny arising from the despotic actions of its "Mutiny-on-the-Bounty" type captain. It was also assumed by many that the *Cyclops* had simply been betrayed to the enemy by its German-born captain, who had changed his last name from the German Wichmann to the less Teutonic sounding Worley. In effect, evidence was indicated for some or all of these possibilities, especially since the *Cyclops,* on leaving port in Barbados, had abruptly turned south instead of north to its announced destination, and then, just as abruptly, disappeared. But eventual examination of German naval records indicated that there were no German submarines or mines in the area at that time. However, a British ship, also incredibly named the *Cyclops,* had been sunk by U-Boats in the North Atlantic. The U.S.S. *Cyclops* at the time of its disappearance was carrying a cargo of manganese ore, and some time after the war, German agents in South America took credit (a phenomenon not unknown in intelligence circles when an operation is successful) for having placed time bombs in the cargo.

At all events the case of the *Cyclops* possesses all the ingredients for a scenario of mystery and adventure—a German captain of a U. S. Navy vessel who may also have been mentally deranged, since he habitually walked the bridge dressed in long underwear and a derby hat; passengers including the former U.S. consul general to Brazil, plus three naval seamen prisoners under indictment for murder, and a couple of AWOL marines.

A theory for the disappearance of the *Cyclops* (which may have furnished an idea for the story of a 1973 movie, *The Poseidon Adventure*) was advanced by U. S. Vice Admiral M. S. Tisdall, who published his opinion, based on the vessel's tendency to roll, in an article entitled "Did the Cyclops Turn Turtle?" In the movie the passenger ship turns turtle, as a result of poor loading and excessive speed, when it is struck by a tidal wave, but does not sink. As far as can be ascertained, the *Cyclops* was not in a hurricane but, of course, could have been struck by a sudden seiche wave, turned over, and gone straight to the bottom, pulling down escaping crew members and equipment in her vortex.

But the only sure thing known about the *Cyclops* is that it vanished—as have so many other ships, large and small, within the Bermuda Triangle. In the words of a Navy fact sheet on the U.S.S. *Cyclops:*

> . . . Since her departure [from Barbados, March 4, 1918] there has been no trace of the vessel. The disappearance of the ship has been one of the most baffling mysteries in the annals of the Navy, all attempts to locate her have proved unsuccessful. . . . Many theories have been advanced, but none that satisfactorily accounts for her disappearance. . . .

However mysterious its disappearance, the vanishing *Cylops* had a noteworthy effect upon future events. It was the factor directly responsible for the establishment of the national strategic stockpile, established several years after the incident. During prior debates in Congress the *Cyclops,* which had disappeared carrying a cargo of manganese, necessary for the production of steel used in weapons and armaments, was cited as a prime example of the necessity for a stockpile, since it illustrated that the United States could not depend on sea lanes for the shipment of strategic materials during international conflicts.

Among the more recent peacetime disappearances of warships in the vicinity of the Bermuda Triangle, the case of the Brazilian warship *São Paulo* is particularly striking. The *São Paulo,* destined for scrapping and carrying a caretaker crew of only eight, was in tow by two oceangoing tugs southwest of the Azores. It suddenly vanished during the night of October 3–4, 1951. Because of a rough sea one of the tugs had released its lines during the night of October 3. However, with the dawn of October 4 and with the sudden return of calm to the sea, the cables on the second tug were noted to be broken or severed and the *São Paulo* was missing. The resultant search by air and surface craft for the warship was characterized by unusual reports: unexplained lights had been seen during the night and early morning and then, on the following day, planes reported dark forms or masses sighted at sea level which soon disappeared. No signs of the *São Paulo* or of its caretaker crew were ever found.

Most commentators on the happenings within the Bermuda Triangle are contented to present them simply as an unsolvable mystery, although several of the most pertinacious researchers have considered that the unexplained disappearances of planes, ships, and people are due to intelligent terrestrial or extraterrestrial agencies, a belief shared, perhaps for want of any other logical explanation, by an increasing number of observers.

One theory, as suggested by both Ivan Sanderson and Dr. Manson Valentine, presupposes the actions of intelligent beings based beneath the sea, while another, more popular theory, of which John Spencer, himself a member of the U. S. Air Force for ten years, is a leading exponent, deduces that extraterrestrials periodically visit the earth and kidnap or "spacenap" men and equipment to ascertain the stage of our technological advancement. They do this not to see if we have advanced far enough, but to ascertain when we are in danger of advancing too far. Although these theories will again be considered in following pages, it is interesting in view of this suggestion of the possibility of an outer (or inner) space research laboratory, to apply this theory to the disappearance of naval vessels and subsequently of aircraft. The spacing of the dates of disappearances as well as the shift of disappearances from naval ships to military planes as well as the variety of ships and pleasure craft that have disappeared, some carrying only people and others with special cargoes, and again some curious incidents connected with these later losses, are apt to give rise, when considered within the framework of this theory, to some rather disquieting thoughts.

Among commercial ships one of the first recorded mysteries in this area concerned the *Rosalie,* a French ship bound for Havana in 1840. The *Rosalie* did not, however, disappear. The crew and passengers disappeared instead, leaving the ship unmanned (except for one canary), with her sails set and cargo intact. If this was a case of piracy, whoever caused the crew and passengers to vanish seemed to have greater interest in the living people on board than in the ship or its cargo. And if sudden sickness or plague had caused the loss of passengers and crew there would have been some indication of such a situation. (As an example of how sudden sickness can cause a ship to become a derelict, there is the case of an incident during the slaving days in the Sargasso Sea, when a schooner sighted a slaver which was sailing erratically. Hailed by the schooner, the slaver's captain asked for help. It seemed that all the slaves and the crew had been stricken by a virulent disease causing blindness. Their call for help was refused by the would-be rescue ship, which departed from the area as quickly as possible, leaving the slaver and its crew and slaves to their doom.)

On February 26, 1855, the *James B. Chester,* a three-master, was found by the *Marathon* sailing aimlessly without crew but with her sails set, within the Sargasso Sea. Investigations of the ship's cabin showed tables and chairs knocked over and in disarray and personal belongings strewn about. The ship's cargo was intact and the lifeboats in place. There was no evidence of bloodshed or attack. The crew had simply vanished, either by being taken off the ship or by the unlikely possibility of having jumped overboard. It was noted by the *Marathon* boarders, however, that the papers and compass of the *James B. Chester* were missing.

An almost unbelieveable incident happened in 1881 to the American schooner *Ellen Austin*. While sailing west of the Azores, this schooner encountered an abandoned schooner which, upon being boarded, proved to be shipshape, with sails furled and with rigging intact. The captain of the *Ellen Austin* took advantage of this windfall by putting a prize crew aboard the derelict. Before the crew could get it under way, however, a sudden squall caused the two ships to break contact and two days passed before the derelict was sighted again. When it was again boarded, it was discovered that the prize crew had vanished, with no indication of what had happened or where they had gone. But the captain of the *Ellen Austin* was persistent and, after considerable reticence on the part of his crew for volunteers, finally persuaded a new prize crew to man the mysterious and apparently dangerous ship. Shortly thereafter another squall came up; contact was again lost and neither the vessel nor the second prize crew was ever seen again. A comparison suggests itself here between the abandoned ship and a trap, with even the sudden squalls fitting into the picture, if the whole idea were not so *outré*.

Inexplicably, deserted ships in the Triangle area have appeared on numerous other occasions. The German bark *Freya,* sailing from Manzanillo, Cuba, to ports in Chile in October 1902, was found abandoned and listing, with the pages of the ship's calendar torn off until October 4.

At this point in time a violent earthquake had taken place in Mexico, and it has been predicated that a seismic shock caused the formation of a huge tidal wave which swept away the crew of the *Freya* or perhaps partially capsized it, and that it subsequently partially righted itself again when the sea was calm.

Tales of empty ships found in the Sargasso Sea or neighboring parts of the Atlantic almost invariably mention the *Mary Celeste,* perhaps the sea's most famous derelict. The incident did not occur in the Sargasso Sea, although the *Mary Celeste* passed north of it on her way to the spot north of the Azores where she was found by a British brig, the *Dei Gratia,* in November 1872. The latter vessel, noting the erratic course of the *Mary Celeste,* hailed her and, obtaining no reply, boarded her and subsequently took the *Mary Celeste* as a prize. The boarding party found her sails were set and her cargo of casks of alcohol was safely stowed in the hold. There were sufficient supplies of food and water but her complement of ten persons had disappeared, including the captain, his wife, and baby daughter. Money, pipes, personal possessions, and even the ship's log were left aboard, although the sextant was missing. The main cabin had been boarded up as if someone had wished to create a stronghold to repel attackers.

This mystery of the sea has been retold and embroidered, been the subject of court trials and investigations, but still has not been solved. The disappearance of the crew has been variously explained as attack of pirates, mutiny and flight after killing the captain, fear of a cargo about to explode, or sudden knowledge of a contraband and dangerous cargo, an outbreak of plague, or hijacking by supposed friends. Lloyds of London, who paid the insurance, inclines to the theory that a sudden but short fire of the alcohol cargo may have frightened the crew off the ship and then gone out, given the properties of alcohol for sudden flare-up, burning with a blue flame, and then extinguishing itself. By the time the short flare-up subsided, the crew may have been unable to return to the ship from the lifeboat. Another possible explanation of irrational behavior on the part of the crew might consist in the presence of ergot in the bread among the ship's stores. Bread tainted with the growth of ergot has affected crews in the past, causing violent madness and death preceded by irrational behavior. A collective insanity brought on by this condition might have induced abandonment of the ship in panic and may explain some other crew disappearances on "ghost ships" in various seas of the world.

Harold Wilkins in *Strange Mysteries of Time and Space* makes a good case for the possibility of the ship's having been boarded and taken at sea by persons already known to the ship's complement, with the implication that the crew was disposed of and the empty ship then "rediscovered" at sea and taken as a prize.

In developing this theory, Wilkins points out the many inconsistencies in the stories of the captain and the crew of the *Dei Gratia,* and the fact that the *Dei Gratia* was moored alongside the *Mary Celeste* for over a week in New York harbor, and sailed shortly after the ill-fated vessel's departure.

After prize proceedings, the refurbished *Mary Celeste* went to sea again but soon acquired the reputation of being a "jinx ship," causing misfortune, destruction, and death among those who sailed on her, until her final master, Captain Gilman Parker, after supplying over-generous liquor rations to all hands and above all to himself, deliberately, it is said, sailed the *Mary Celeste* onto a rocky reef near Haiti and so ended her unlucky career.

Other deserted ships with less indications of what happened to their crews include the *Carol Deering,* which ran aground in February 1921 on the North Carolina shore with no indication of what had happened to the crew except that they had abandoned or been taken off the ship while a meal was about to be served; the *John and Mary,* found deserted in April 1932 fifty miles south of Bermuda; the *Gloria Colite,* a 125-foot schooner found deserted at sea on February 3, 1940; and the *Rubicon,* a Cuban vessel found abandoned (except for a hungry dog) off Key Largo, Florida, on October 22, 1944. The last entry in her log was for September 26 and noted that the ship was then in Havana harbor. Missing lifeboats suggested that the crew had left in a hurry. Ivan Sanderson has observed that in cases of a crew abandoning a ship it is most unusual for them not to take the ship's mascot or their own individual pets. It is suggested that the crew was forcibly removed, perhaps by entities who wanted only specimens capable of oral communication. Sanderson further comments that it is worthy of note that while cats, dogs, and canaries have been found on ships from which the crews have disappeared ". . . parrots seem to vanish with the humans . . ." perhaps, one might imagine, because coherent (or incoherent) speech is an easy way to recognize the dominant species of the planet Earth.

Crews and passengers have frequently vanished from many smaller boats, later found abandoned and adrift, such as the yacht *Connemara IV*, found 400 miles southwest of Bermuda in September 1955, empty of passengers and crew; the sixty-foot *Maple Bank*, found drifting north of Bermuda on June 30, 1969, with no trace of survivors; *The Vagabond*, a twelve-meter owner-operated yacht found adrift but otherwise ship-shape west of the Azores on July 6, 1969, with no sign of its owner, Captain Wallace P. Williams, or its crew. Some boats have disappeared on fairly short trips, such as the case of Al Snyder, a well-known jockey, who took several of his friends on his cabin cruiser out of Miami on March 5, 1948, to go fishing at Sandy Key and, although the yacht was later found, the occupants had disappeared.

While certain abandoned small boats found on the high seas after the Cuban Revolution may have had something to do with the activities of escaping Cubans and those pursuing them, one striking disappearance had nothing to do with the Cuban situation.

The incident of the *Witchcraft* is an outstanding example of lightninglike sudden disappearance of a small craft not only within sight of its port but while located at one of the harbor's buoys. Dan Burack, owner of *Witchcraft,* which, incidentally, was reputed to be "unsinkable," had invited a priest, Father Pat Hogan, to see the Christmas lights of Miami from offshore on Christmas Eve 1967. They proceeded through calm seas to about one mile from the shore and stopped to admire the lights from the vicinity of buoy number 7. At this point Burack made a single unexpected call for help to the Coast Guard, giving his exact position. It took an alerted Coast Guard vessel only twenty minutes to reach buoy number 7 but when it arrived there was no sign of the *Witchcraft.* When the search was finally suspended, a Coast Guard spokesman stated, somewhat paradoxically: "We presume they are missing— but not lost at sea."

The list of cargo ships, fishing vessels and pleasure craft that have vanished with their crews is impressive. Most of the ships have disappeared in good weather and have left no floating wreckage, oil slicks, lifeboats, life jackets (with one notable exception), or bodies, either in the sea or washed up on neighboring beaches. Like the disappearing planes, the ships sent no SOS messages and reported nothing wrong over their transmitters.

These vanishing ships have included the *Cotopaxi,* a freighter bound for Havana from Charleston in 1925; the *Suduffco,* a freighter sailing south from Port Newark in 1926; the *Stavenger,* in 1931 with forty-three persons on board, which was last located south of Cat Island; and the freighter *Anglo-Australian* in March 1938, with a crew of thirty-nine, which radioed, "All well," as it passed the Azores on its way west.

A spectacular last radio message was received from

the Japanese freighter *Raifuku Maru,* presumably at the time of its disappearance between the Bahamas and Cuba during the winter 1924. The words of the radio message were an unusual call for help: "Danger like a dagger now. . . . Come quickly. . . . We cannot escape. . . ." without, however, specifying what the danger was. If the danger was a sudden storm or unexpected waterspout, it would seem normal for a radio officer to give precise information which might later serve to aid rescue operations, rather than to indulge in imaginative comparisons, however striking.

Lost ships in the Atlantic during the war years had varied and sufficient reasons, including submarines, mines, bombs, and sabotage, to be lost without trace —but considerably after the war, large ships continued to disappear within the Bermuda Triangle area. The freighter *Sandra,* bound for Puerto Cabello from Savannah in June 1950, carrying a cargo of insecticide, passed by St. Augustine, Florida, in good weather, and thereafter all contact was lost and never re-established. It is of interest, in the case of the S.S. *Sandra* and others, that most of the American ships lost have disappeared in sight of land. Farther south the *Sno' Boy,* a fishing vessel with forty persons on board, was lost without trace or explanation in 1963 between Kingston, Jamaica, and Northeast Cay.

Among the many pleasure boats reported as missing without trace within the area (perhaps an average of one per month) the case of the *Revonoc,* a forty-six-foot racing yacht, which had won prizes in the Newport–Bermuda race, which disappeared during a short cruise between Key West and Fort Lauderdale between Christmas and New Year of 1967 (a fatal time, as we have seen before, for disappearances) caused particular comment for several reasons. In the first place the yacht was designed for racing in all weather. Secondly, Captain Conover (the name *Revonoc* was Conover spelled backward), skipper and owner, was an excellent sailor and Commodore of the Cruising Club of America, "too good a sailor" to risk an accident on such a relatively short cruise. In any case, since he was sailing so close to land, some vestige of the yacht would have been found along the shore had it struck a reef. In an attempt to give some logic for the *Revonoc*'s disappearance, the then yachting editor of the New York *Herald Tribune* suggested the possibility that a freighter, known to be in the area at the time, had simply run over the yacht at night, sending it and its crew to the bottom without notice or trace.

More than half a century before Conover's disappearance on the *Revonoc*, another well-known sailor, Joshua Slocum, the first man to circumnavigate the world solo, undertook a second voyage in 1909 on his thirty-seven-foot yawl, *The Spray*. He was reported to have entered the Triangle area, sailing south from Miami, and shortly afterward, he and *The Spray* disappeared forever.

The disappearance of small and medium-sized craft within the Triangle is no doubt due in many cases to weather conditions, especially in the winter, when they become even more unpredictable than usual when the cold Arctic air masses meet the warm air from the tropics. This could have been the case with the schooner *Windfall* (fifty-six feet, disappeared off Bermuda in 1962), the fifty-five-foot *Evangeline* (en route from Miami to the Bahamas, 1962), the fifty-eight-foot *Enchantress* (disappeared en route from Charleston to St. Thomas, 1946), and the thirty-six-foot ketch *Danc-*

ing Feather (disappeared between Nassau and North Carolina, 1964), all of which occurred in winter months, when large waves whipped up by unexpected storms could have caused a small craft to founder even before a radio message could be sent. But this, of course, would not explain the disappearance of ships in relatively calm waters, or the several occasions when large freighters or Navy ships have disappeared without a trace.

The loss of a 425-foot freighter, the *Marine Sulphur Queen,* with a crew of thirty-nine, on or about February 2, 1963, is particularly striking because of the size of the vessel. It was bound for Norfolk, Virginia, from Beaumont, Texas, with a cargo of 15,000 long tons of molten sulphur carried in steel tanks. The weather was good. The ship was last heard of from a point near Dry Tortugas, in the Gulf of Mexico, an area in or near the Triangle according to its somewhat elastic boundaries.

Paradoxically, the vessel was first missed not by its owners but by a brokerage house because of a chain of unusual circumstances. One of the seamen on the *Marine Sulphur Queen* had been speculating in the stock market, specifically in wheat futures, a pastime that normally requires rather close contact with one's broker, and had placed a "buy" order before the ship left port. The brokerage house had executed the order and had cabled him confirmation. When no response was received, the brokerage house informed the ship's owners that they could not reach the vessel: the first indication that all was not well and the incident that initiated the unsuccessful search for the *Marine Sulphur Queen,* launched by the Coast Guard on February 6. Its planes and ships ranged from the Virginia capes to the eastern part of the Gulf of Mexico. Although the search was discontinued on February 15, five days later the Navy reported finding a life jacket from the *Marine Sulphur Queen* fifteen miles out at sea, south of Key West. This initiated a new hunt, which found only another life jacket. A subsequent investigation dealt with a wide range of possibilities: explosion of the sulphur; capsizing; hitting a mine; or even capture and confiscation by Cubans (or Cuban sympathizers). A Marine Board of Investigation noted that the *Marine Sulphur Queen* had "disappeared at sea without the transmission of a radio distress message," but offered neither solution nor theory concerning this disaster.

Stories about the Bermuda Triangle were once more revived when the atomic submarine U.S.S. *Scorpion,* carrying a crew of ninety-nine, failed to return to its home port in Norfolk, Virginia, on May 28, 1968. It had sent its last routine message back to its base on May 21 from 250 miles west of the Azores. On June 5 it was presumed lost, but several months later a naval oceanographic research ship located some wreckage 460 miles south of the Azores, at a depth of more than 10,000 feet. As underwater photographs seem to have established the identity of the *Scorpion,* it cannot be said to have vanished, although the reason for its loss on the edge of the Sargasso Sea cannot be ascertained. If there is, as some investigators of the Bermuda Triangle phenomena have suggested, an intelligence-directed reason behind many of the disappearances or near disappearances, the loss of several atomic submarines in the western Atlantic suggests wider possibilities than equipment malfunction.

If the area of disappearing ships is projected into the Gulf of Mexico, as John Spencer suggests, a 1966 disappearance of a vessel there would also be considered, especially in view of a later to be discussed escape from whatever menace ships and planes are facing in this area. It concerns the sixty-seven-foot tugboat *Southern Cities,* which left Freeport, Texas, on October 29, 1966, with a 210-foot barge in tow. When the *Southern Cities* did not make its daily report by radio, an air search was initiated which located the barge, complete and with its cargo of chemicals undisturbed, with its towline intact up to its connection chain—but no tugboat or tugboat crew. An excerpt from the report of the Maritime Board of Inquiry of the Coast Guard might be applied to any or all of the numerous planes and ships that have disappeared: ". . . the failure of the vessel to transmit a distress message appears to justify the conclusion that the loss of the vessel may have occurred so rapidly as to preclude the transmission of such a message."

More recent disappearances include the *Ithaca Island,* in November 1968, carring a cargo of grain from Norfolk to Manchester; the *Milton Iatrides,* in April 1970, en route from New Orleans to Capetown with a cargo of vegetable oils and caustic soda; and the *Anita,* a large cargo ship (20,000 tons) with a crew of thirty-two, which sailed from Newport News in March 1973, with a cargo of coal for Germany and was not heard from again. After a characteristically thorough investigation, definitely establishing that the *Anita* had inexplicably disappeared, Lloyds of London paid $3,000,000 insurance to the owners of the *Anita.*

The *Anita*'s sister ship, the *Norse Variant,* which left port within two hours before her, radioed that she was sinking 150 miles southeast of Cape May. It was thought at first that all crew members were lost, but one survivor saved himself by clinging to a wooden hatch. He reported that the sinking occurred within minutes; an extremely violent wind suddenly rose, blowing movable objects from the decks. Suddenly heavy seas swamped the ship, filling the holds, and sinking the ship within five minutes.

Considering the diversity of the cargoes of the many merchant ships that have vanished, there seems to be no underlying theme suggesting a connection between the cargo and the disappearance, such as piracy, danger of explosives, mutiny, and the like. They seem to be random disappearances, but concentrated within the same area.

In commenting on the disappearance of ships and planes within the Bermuda Triangle, an information officer of the U. S. Third Naval District has expressed a widely held, although certainly unofficial professional opinion: "It's been a real mystery. Nobody in the Navy sneers at this thing. We've always known there's something strange about this Bermuda Triangle. But nobody has ever found out what it is. There doesn't seem to be any physical or logical reason. It's almost as if these ships had been suddenly covered by some sort of electronic camouflage net."

With only a few exceptions, almost all of the incidents concerned with planes and ships have taken place in, or in the vicinity of, the Sargasso Sea and the coastal waters which border it. Ivan Sanderson, while warning about concentrating area research on any "glaring incident," comments on the "aggravating aspects" of the fact that (the position of) the Sargasso Sea just about coincides with the fact that ". . . most of the disappearances of the planes and most of the ships of old . . . had occurred in this mysterious lozenge-shaped area . . ."

It would seem to be an ironic coincidence that this area, feared from ancient times in legends that existed long before it was officially discovered and later feared for hundreds of years as a sea of doom, should conserve its sinister aura and much of its mystery right into the space age, uniting in wonder individuals who might be termed the opposite ends of an exploration spectrum—Columbus and the astronauts of Apollo 12.

Columbus, on board the *Santa Maria,* was the first observer we have on record to notice the unexplained glowing in the sea, the luminous white water of the Bahamas, near the western edges of the Sargasso Sea, which he saw on his first voyage on October 11, 1492, two hours after sunset, while the astronauts noted these same luminous streaks or flumes in the water as the last lights visible to them from the earth. This phenomenon has been variously supposed to be marl stirred up by bonefish, banks of fish, or other organic matter. Whatever its origin, still unexplained, this strange light is visible from the surface and especially noticeable from the air.

Columbus' first voyage was the occasion for other mysterious incidents which even today are still a source of comment and wonder in the Triangle area. On September 15, 1492, while within the western part of the Sargasso Sea, he and his increasingly nervous crew observed a huge bolt of fire shoot across the heavens and fall or disappear into the ocean. Some days later, members of his crew were again filled with dread by an inexplicable disturbance affecting the ship's compass, an odd forecast, on the eve of the discovery of the

New World, of the electromagnetic disturbances still affecting air and sea navigation within the Triangle.

Still another of the several mysteries connected with the Sargasso Sea, and one that has intrigued ancient as well as modern observers, concerns the spawning of eels. Aristotle (384–322 B.C.) was the first naturalist of antiquity reported to have brought up the puzzling question of the breeding grounds of the European eels, which were, of course, the only eels he knew about. The eels were known to leave their ponds, lakes, streams, and small rivers and swim down the large rivers that empty into the sea. This was all that was known about the breeding grounds of the eels until about 2,500 years later when a Danish scientist, Dr. Johannes Schmidt, discovered where the eels had been going on their journeys during all the intervening centuries since the question was first raised.

The adult European eels follow the waterways that empty into the Atlantic; there they unite and swim in a great shoal, progressing slowly for about four months, accompanied by flights of feeding gulls and packs of sharks, until they reach the point in the Sargasso Sea where they stop and spawn at a considerable depth. There the adults die and the newly born eels start their long trip back, borne by the Gulf Stream on a return trip to Europe which takes about two years to accomplish.

The behavior of eels from the American continent follows the same pattern in reverse. These eels swim eastward and meet the European eels in the depths of the Sargasso Sea, and the young eels return to their ancestral homes in the Americas. This remarkable behavior of eels and their inherited nostophylia (memory of an ancestral home or breeding place) has given rise to some extremely interesting theories, including the one that their original breeding ground was in a great river of a former continent which once existed in the Atlantic, in the vicinity of the Sargasso Sea, and that the eels still seek out their original spawning grounds at the site of the vanished river which once flowed through a continent now thousands of feet under the sea. It has even been suggested that the weeds of the Sargasso Sea are adapted underwater growing remnants of the vegetation of the former Atlantic continent which sank, according to historic legend, with great rapidity, taking with it all its luxuriant forests and greenery.

But of the several mysteries of the Sargasso Sea and its borders, that of the lost ships and planes and their possible connection with other phenomena is the most intriguing, especially since it concerns an area so widely traveled every day by so many sea and aircraft. It may be, of course, that there is a logical explanation for every one of the disappearances and that terms like "atmospheric aberrations," "holes in the sky," "disintegration through unexplained turbulence," "sky traps," "a gravity sink," and implications that aircraft and large and small ships have been captured and removed by unknown agencies, simply represent attempts to explain the unexplainable.

There is, however, another element to the mystery— a rather recent and unexpected one. In the many past disappearances in the Bermuda Triangle, there have been not only no survivors, but not a single body among the many victims has been recovered. However, within recent years, with the spread of the Bermuda Triangle legend, certain pilots and seamen are beginning to lose their understandable reticence to discuss the unusual and to tell of escapes that they personally have had from forces operating within the Bermuda Triangle. A consideration of some of these accounts indicates a possible pattern which may explain how (if not why) some of these losses have occurred.

4

Some Who Escaped

IN HIS BOOK "INVISIBLE HORIZONS," A COMPENDIUM of mysteries of the sea, Vincent Gaddis, in a special section devoted to the Bermuda Triangle ("The Triangle of Death") recounts that shortly after he wrote his original article on the Bermuda Triangle in 1964, an article that apparently gave it its name, he received a letter from an ex-airman named Dick Stern containing pertinent and surprising information. Stern wrote that toward the end of 1944 he had taken part in a flight destined for Italy. The flight consisted of a group of seven bombers and, about three hundred miles off Bermuda, his plane suddenly experienced such unexpected and violent turbulence that it had to return to the United States. When this occurred the weather was clear and the stars were visible, but the turbulence caused the plane to turn over and to pitch so violently that the crew was thrown to the ceiling. The turbulence caused the plane to lose altitude to a point where it was almost forced into the sea. When his plane returned to base he learned that only one other plane had returned from a flight of seven, and there had been no radio contact with the others and no subsequent survivors or wreckage located. This incident, which happened a year *before* the loss of Flight 19, also in December, was not considered as an unusual loss, since it occurred in wartime and was given no publicity.

Some years after the war, Stern and his wife were on a daytime flight from Bermuda to Nassau in a Bristol Britannia when a somewhat similar happening occurred. By a curious coincidence, Mrs. Stern was, at that very moment, talking about the previous incident. Suddenly the plane dropped without warning, the food which the passengers were eating hit the ceiling, and the plane shook violently. It continued to shake and to rise and fall for a quarter of an hour.

This phenomenon may be an example of "clear air turbulence" (CAT), which, if intensive or prolonged enough, would possibly cause some planes to be shaken apart and scattered over the sea. In any case Dick Stern has the distinction of having encountered the same unexpected and menacing force twice at almost the same place in the Triangle—and lived to tell about it.

Joe Talley, captain of a fishing boat, the *Wild Goose,* experienced a different, though not, in his case at least, fatal way of disappearing within the Triangle. It did not concern a plane but his own boat, in tow behind another boat, on the surface of the sea. The locale of his experience was the Tongue of the Ocean, an extremely deep area within the Bahama group, but not part of the Bahama Banks, in that its relatively small area is thousands of feet deep; a precipitous drop-off directly east of Andros Island, and the site of many disappearances.

Captain Talley's sixty-five-foot shark-fishing vessel was to be towed south in the Tongue of the Ocean by the 104-foot *Caicos Trader*. The weather was good, with a brisk trade wind coming from the southwest. The two vessels were approaching the southern section of the Tongue of the Ocean, where this submarine canyon emerges into a great craterlike hole at its south end with a diameter of forty miles. Reefs and the Exuma chain to the east protect the Tongue of the Ocean at this point from excessively high seas that might develop from southeast trade winds. It was nighttime and Captain Talley was asleep in his bunk below decks. Suddenly he was awakened by a flood of water pouring over him. He automatically grabbed a life jacket and fought his way to an open porthole. As he forced his way out, he found he was under water but he encountered a line and followed it to the surface, a distance calculated as being from fifty to eighty feet. He had apparently been submerged to a distance of forty to fifty feet when he escaped from his quarters.

When he got to the end of the line, and the surface, he found that the *Caicos Trader* had continued on its way without him. What had happened was that the sudden force which was drawing the *Wild Goose* under water toward the bottom, with Captain Talley on board, was threatening to capsize the *Caicos Trader* because of the connecting towline. The crew of the towboat cut the towline, left the immediate area, and then turned about to see if by some miracle Talley had managed to escape from the cabin of his craft as it was drawn down beneath the sea. The crew of the towboat had seen the *Wild Goose* go straight down "as if in a whirlpool."

After about half an hour, Talley, now about to sink, was surprised to hear his name shouted over the water by megaphone from the now-returned *Caicos Trader*. He was able to shout a reply and was subsequently rescued. As most captains in the area are familiar with the many unexplained losses of craft often accompanied by compass and radio malfunction, inquiry was made concerning the behavior of the compass during the incident. It was found, however, that the helmsman had set the course and had left the wheel during the incident, so there was no way of telling if there had been a mechanical aberration at that time.

Other boats have lost their tows in the area, sometimes losing the crew as well on the boat they were towing, unlike Captain Talley, who lived to tell about his experience. In some cases what seems to be a fog has covered the second ship and there has been malfunction of compass and electrical equipment on the first ship. One wonders why there are reports from towboats about these forces and not from single boats. Perhaps this is because single boats simply disappear—without witness—while towboats are close enough—at the end of a line—to observe what is happening.

The experience of Captain Don Henry, in 1966, gives a graphic account of a "tug of war" between the towboat and an unidentified force attempting, consciously or unconsciously, to capture the barge.

Captain Henry is the owner of a salvage company in Miami called the Sea Phantom Exploration Company, and he has had many years experience as a sea captain, navigator, and both a hard hat and free diver. He is about fifty-five years old, heavy, with a powerful chest and arms befitting a longtime diver. He gives the impression of being extremely solid and muscular and, for a heavy man, moves with surprising lightness and speed. To make a point, he will bring one fist into the cup of his other hand or make an illustrative gesture which gives one the impression that it would not be good to find oneself on the receiving end of his fist. His eyes, accustomed to watching the sea, are frank and penetrating. His certainty in his conversation and recall of detail make it pertinent to let Captain Henry recount the incident in his own words, noted during a conversation concerning the disappearing barge.

. . . We were coming in on the return trip between Puerto Rico and Fort Lauderdale. We had been out for three days towing an empty barge which had carried petroleum nitrate. I was aboard the *Good News,* a hundred-and-sixty-foot-long tug of two thousand horsepower. The barge we were towing weighted twenty-five hundred tons and was on a line a thousand feet behind. We were on the Tongue of the Ocean, after coming through the Exumas. The depth was about six hundred fathoms.

It was afternoon, the weather was good, and the sky was clear. I had gone to the cabin in back of the bridge for a few minutes when I heard a lot of hollering going on. I came out of the cabin onto the bridge and yelled, "What the hell is going on?" The first thing I looked at was the compass, which was spinning clockwise. There was no reason that this should ever happen—the only place besides here I ever heard it to happen was in the St. Lawrence River at Kingston, where a big deposit of iron or maybe a meteorite on the bottom makes the compasses go crazy. I did not know what had happened, but something big was sure as hell going on. The water seemed to be coming from all directions. The horizon disappeared—we couldn't see where the horizon was—the water, sky, and horizon all blended together. We couldn't see where we were.

Whatever was happening robbed, stole, or borrowed everything from our generators. All electric appliances and outlets ceased to produce power. The generators were still running, but we weren't getting any power. The engineer tried to start an auxiliary generator but couldn't get a spark.

I was worried about the tow. It was tight but I couldn't see it. It seemed to be covered by a cloud, and around it the waves seemed to be more choppy than in other areas.

I rammed the throttles full ahead. I couldn't see where we were going, but I wanted to get the hell out in a hurry. It seemed that something wanted to pull us back, but it couldn't quite make it.

Coming out of it was like coming out of a fog bank. When we came out the towline was sticking out straight—like the Indian rope trick—with nothing visible at the end of it where it was covered by a fog concentrated around it. I jumped to the main deck and pulled. The damned barge came out from the fog, but there was no fog any place else. In fact I could see for eleven miles. In the foggy area where the tow should have been, the water was confused, although the waves were not big. Call me Nero, not Hero—I wasn't going back to find out what it was that was back there.

Have you ever felt two people pulling on your arms in opposite directions? It felt that we were on a place or point that somebody or something wanted, and somebody or something wanted us to be in another place from where we were going.

QUESTION: *Was there a greenish appearance to the horizon?*

No, it was milky. That's all I can say. I wasn't looking for colors. After we left the batteries had to be recharged. I had to throw away fifty flashlight batteries.

Did you think of the Bermuda Triangle?

Yes. It was the only thing I could think of at that time. I thought—My God! I am another statistic!

Did you ever have other experiences like this?

No. I've heard other people have and that one tow was lost with the people on it, and with the tow cable cut. But this was the only experience I had. Once was plenty!

Jim Richardson, a former Navy pilot, is now president of the Chalk Air Ferry Service operating between Opa-Locka Airport in Miami and Bimini and other points in the Bahamas. As president of the most important passenger service in the area and an outstanding promoter of Bimini, he maintains what may be termed a non-committal attitude about the alleged menace of the Bermuda Triangle. He expresses one local reaction to the spread of the legend with a pilot's pithy directness:

It's something people don't talk about. They say you're out of your God-damned mind.

Nevertheless, in his numerous flights to the Bahamas, he too has encountered electronic and magnetic aberrations. On an early morning flight from Florida to Turks Islands, accompanied by his son, the plane's compass suddenly started to spin from left to right. He asked his son, "What's wrong with the compass?" To which the son replied, as a perfectly natural explanation, "We are over Andros." He observed that this has frequently happened "every time we go over deep waters in front of Moselle Reef." This reef, incidentally, is a place often noted for the presence of mysterious lights shining at night, and among the fishermen of Bimini, has the reputation of being "haunted." These lights on the reef have also been observed by the same Jim Richardson and other pilots of planes and ships.

A more pronounced electronic incident is recounted by Chuck Wakeley, wherein an electronic force or presence seemed temporarily to take possession of his plane while he was flying between Nassau and Fort Lauderdale. Chuck Wakeley is about thirty years old and has been a professional pilot of planes and helicopters for over ten years. He has had considerable flying experience, much of it solo over the jungles of Panama and South America, where a good memory for details and a cool reaction for emergencies are often the secrets of survival.

He is a trained observer and holds a high security clearance from the United States Government. Talking to him one is impressed by his sincerity and his effort to recount his experience exactly as it happened. He is an expressive speaker, and it is interesting to note that he had not heard of the Bermuda Triangle as such until after his experience.

In November of 1964 I was a pilot for Sunline Aviation in Miami. During this time I took a charter flight to Nassau to drop off some people and return. I dropped off the passengers and left Nassau Airport shortly after dark. The weather was very clear and the stars were shining. I was tracking outbound on the Nassau VOR [variable omnirange] to intercept the Bimini VOR en route. At about 9:30 P.M. I passed the northern tip of Andros Island and could see the lights of some of the settlements.

I had leveled off at about eight thousand feet and was settling back for a routine flight but, thirty to fifty miles past Andros, on a direct heading for Bimini, I began to notice something unusual: a very faint glowing effect on the wings. At first I thought it was an illusion created by the cockpit lights shining through the tinted Plexiglas windows because the wings had a translucent appearance, appearing pale blue-green, although they were actually painted bright white.

In the course of about five minutes this glow increased in intensity until it became so bright that I had great difficulty reading my instruments. My magnetic compass began revolving, slowly but steadily; the fuel gauges, which had read "half full" at take off, now read "full." My electric auto pilot suddenly put the aircraft into a hard right turn, and I had to shut it off and operate manually. I could not trust any of the electrically run instruments, as they were either totally out or behaving erratically. Soon the whole aircraft was glowing, but it was not a reflected glow, since the glow was coming from the aircraft itself. When I looked out the window at the wings I remember noticing that they were not only glowing bluish-green but also looked fuzzy.

At this point I could no longer rely on my gyro, horizon, or altitude indicators, and, since it was night and I was flying with an artificial horizon, I had no horizon to go by. The glow was so intense that I could no longer see the stars. I did the only thing I could—that was to let go of the controls, and let the craft fly on whatever heading it would take. The glow built up to a blinding crescendo of light, lasted for about five minutes, and then diminished gradually.

All instruments began to function normally as soon as the glowing dissipated. I checked all circuit breakers and none had popped. No fuses were blown and I realized that equipment was functioning normally when the fuel gauges returned to reading that the tanks were half full. The magnetic compass became steady and showed that I was only a few degrees off course. I engaged the auto pilot and it was normal. Before landing I checked all systems—landing gear, flaps, and so on. They were all normal. Incidentally the aircraft had static lines and should have drained all static elements.

QUESTION: *Did you think your experience was connected with the Bermuda Triangle?*

I did not know about the Bermuda Triangle until after the incident. I thought what I had seen was St. Elmo's fire in spite of the fact that St. Elmo's fire doesn't act that way.

When did you hear about the Bermuda Triangle?

I heard about it when I started to speak to other pilots about my experience. Things like that have happened to other pilots, but they don't like to talk about it. Anyhow, there's no way to avoid what they call the Triangle if you go to some place like Puerto Rico, unless you fly up north of Bermuda. You hear a lot more about the Triangle now, especially when any completely illogical disappearance of a plane happens.

What may have been a visual observation, seen from the air, of some destructive force within the Triangle was reported in *Pursuit,* a quarterly review published by the Society for the Investigation of the Unexplained. The author of the report, Robert Durand, tells of an incident observed from the control nacelle of a Boeing 707 on a flight from San Juan to New York on April 11, 1963. The location of the sighting was reported as 19°54′ north latitude, 66°47′ west longitude, a point well within the Triangle and over the Puerto Rico Trench, one of the ocean's deepest canyons, where the sea reaches a depth of five and a half miles.

The unusual sighting, first reported by the copilot (anonymous by preference) took place at 1:30 P.M., twenty minutes after takeoff, when the jet was at an altitude of 31,000 feet. The copilot suddenly noticed, about five miles to starboard from the route the jet was following, that the ocean was rising into a great round mound as if from an underwater atomic explosion, and that it looked like "a big cauliflower" in the water. He immediately called the captain's and the flight engineer's attention to it and they observed it in detail for about thirty seconds, and then unfastened their seat belts and climbed over to starboard for a still better view. The roiling titanic mount of water attained, in their judgment, a diameter of half a mile to a mile, with a height of perhaps half its width. Understandably, the captain did not go back for a closer look, but kept to his schedule. As the plane left the area the enormous boiling mound was seen to be beginning to subside. The copilot later checked several agencies, including the Coast Guard and the FBI, as well as a seismic specialist, but received no corroborating information of anything unusual, such as earthquakes, tidal waves, or enormous waterspouts, having transpired in the area.

It has been variously suggested that this apparent atomic explosion may have had something to do with the atomic submarine U.S.S. *Thresher,* which had been lost on the previous day, or its atomic warheads, although the *Thresher* was reported lost thousands of miles away. This theory, of course, would only be valid if important elements in the loss of the *Thresher* had been kept secret (which is possible) or, as has been informally theorized, if a submarine of a potential enemy had been attacked or sunk in retaliation for the *Thresher*'s sinking. But discounting the military hypothesis, the point of occurrence constitutes still another affirmation of the forces at work within the Bermuda Triangle.

Another recent account of what might have been an escape by surface craft was recounted by the participants to Norman Bean, electronic engineer and inventor, whose inventions include closed-circuit underwater television and shark repellent. Norman Bean, a resident of Miami, is a lecturer on UFOs and a close observer of phenomena in the Bermuda Triangle. The incident took place on an evening in September 1972 between Featherbed Banks and Matheson Hammock in Biscayne Bay and concerned a diesel-powered boat with the ominous name of *Nightmare*. The *Nightmare,* carrying three passengers, was returning to port at night, appropriately, from a fishing trip in Biscayne Bay. When it reached the Featherbed Banks area, it was noticed that the compass was off about ninety degrees as compared with the lights of its destination, Coconut Grove. The boat lights became weak and then were extinguished, as if there had been a tremendous drain exerted on the batteries. Thereupon, disregarding the compass reading, the pilot steered directly for landmarks due west, under full power. But the only change in position was to the north, as ascertained by shore lights slipping to the south. For two hours the boat continued toward the shore but was unable to make any progress and seemed, if anything, to be backing up.

During this time, a large dark shape blotting out the stars was noted by the occupants of the boat in the air between the boat and Matheson Hammock, a mile or two to the west. As they watched it they noticed a moving light enter the dark area, remain poised for a few moments, and then disappear. Shortly afterward the dark shape also disappeared. After the disappearance the compass returned to normal, the generator recharged the batteries, and the boat was able to proceed forward.

An almost identical experience was reported to Bean by a member of the audience at one of his lectures given some years prior to the case of the *Nightmare*. The individual, a retired U. S. Navy captain, was unwilling to discuss the incident at the lecture, but later told Bean about it in private, as he, like so many observers of "unexplainable" phenomena, was unwilling to jeopardize his reputation for veracity or exact observation.

The incident happened a week before Christmas 1957. A thirty-five-foot diesel-powered fishing boat belonging to and piloted by the captain on a course to Freeport, in the Bahamas, was unable to proceed forward for a period of several hours and was even pushed backward several miles. The generator went out as well as the lights and radio and the compass went into a spin. Although the diesel engine kept running, the boat was unable to make any headway. As in the case of the *Nightmare,* the crew noted that, although the water was calm and the stars bright, a certain area of the sky, dead ahead on their intended course, showed a starless black patch of regular outline. At one point they saw three moving lights in a row enter this dark area and disappear. Shortly afterward, the black patch in the sky suddenly lifted and the boat was able to resume progress forward, the lights and the battery-operated radio went on, and the compass returned to normal. The captain and his four passengers later learned that during the same night, forty miles away, a freighter that had been navigating the Gulf Stream southward ended up beached on a mudbank to the west, near Fort Lauderdale, its steering device having suffered a ninety-degree deflection.

An incident which happened to a twin-engine Beechcraft on a flight from George Town on Great Exuma, Bahamas, on November 15, 1972, is an interesting example of the capriciousness of these forces and at least one case, if motives and reason can be attributed to them, where they seemed to aid rather than destroy the plane. Dr. S. F. Jablonsky, a Fort Lauderdale psychologist, made the following report to Dr. Manson Valentine, who recalls it as follows:

The plane left George Town at twilight with nine people aboard, including five pilots. The weather was good, the sea was calm, and the visibility was excellent. There was a light breeze from the southeast.

About ten minutes after takeoff when the aircraft was over the Tongue of the Ocean northwest of Exuma, all electrically operated systems, compass, radio, lights, and even hydraulic controls, suddenly and rapidly deteriorated and all batteries drained completely.

The pilot's first reaction was to try to land at New Providence (approximately sixty miles due north) as he could navigate by the setting sun until the lights of Nassau became visible. On second thoughts, however, he remembered that the radio was out and he could not advise the airport of his arrival and he had no lights working to signal his approach. It was therefore decided to head straight for the nearest airstrip on Andros and soon they were able to distinguish the little airport near the south end of the island. For landing in these circumstances, the captain undertook a glide pattern after a turn west of the airstrip to make certain there were no obstructions and to get lined up as accurately as possible with the runway and wind. Since the hydraulic system was not operating, the landing wheels could not be lowered and, of course, there were no landing lights. Dr. Jablonsky later observed that "the plane seemed to be landing as if buoyed up on a cushion of air." The ends of the propellers touched ground first, setting off a shower of sparks but, instead of crashing, the plane settled on the ground. There was no damage to the fuselage and even the low-hanging air scoops were intact.

On the following day two new propellers were sent out to Andros and installed. The plane's batteries were recharged, but even before this the hydraulic system had regained its functions. The flight took off again and arrived at Fort Lauderdale without further incident.

As this book goes to press, the Cunard Liner *Queen Elizabeth 2* has just escaped an appointment with disaster in the upper center of the Bermuda Triangle. On April 3, 1974, due to a breakdown of three of her boilers (attributed to an oil leak), and interruption of electric power, air conditioning, etc., this most modern of superliners lay becalmed, like her predecessor of past ages, in the Sargasso Sea, while the passengers awaited rescue consoled by free, though warm, drinks offered by the line.

In one of the first radio interviews from aboard ship, a professional football player passenger (the cruise was designated "Sun and Fun Pigskin Cruise") said on the air: "The Captain tells me that we are sitting here right in the middle of the Bermuda Triangle." Subsequent reports, however, seemed studiously to avoid any reference to this fateful area.

As a footnote to the incident, it is interesting to note that radar disappearance of the *Queen Elizabeth 2* was reportedly observed by a crew member of a Coast Guard cutter following the vessel. As the *Queen Elizabeth 2,* making 35 knots, entered the Triangle the cutter lost it on radar, although it remained visibly in sight, disappearing shortly thereafter. The cutter's communication with the *Queen Elizabeth 2* and radar contact seemed to be affected from the moment the vessel entered the Triangle. While it has not yet been suggested that the mysterious forces of the Triangle were somehow involved in the *Queen Elizabeth 2* breakdown, it is possible that radar communication with the cutter could have been affected by the known radio and electrical anomalies existent within the Bermuda Triangle.

When we consider the total number of plane and ship disappearances, as well as the pattern of what have apparently been escapes from forces at work within the area of the Bermuda Triangle, we must also consider the possibility of there being a logical explanation or a variety of logical explanations for these happenings. The deeper we go into the problem, however, the more we begin to wonder whether there even exists, within our familiar framework of scientific reference, what might be called a logical explanation.

5

Is There a Logical Explanation?

I T HAS SOMETIMES BEEN POINTED OUT IN MINIMIZING
the importance or even the existence of the Bermuda Triangle that it is not truly a mystery at all in
that, since ships and planes are lost all over the world,
a Triangle projected over any group of important sea
lanes would indicate a disturbing incidence of loss if the
triangle were made large enough. Moreover the ocean
is large, planes and ships relatively small, and the ocean
is perpetually in motion, with both surface and submarine currents. Planes or small boats lost between the
Bahamas and Florida, where the Gulf Stream flows
north at more than four knots an hour, could end up
at such a distance from the point where they were last
reported that they would seem to have effectively disappeared. The speed of this current is, however, well
known to the Coast Guard, whose search and rescue
missions take into account current and wind deviations

in the approximate area where a craft has disappeared. The radius immediately given for complete circular search for a large vessel is five miles, with ten miles for a plane, and fifteen miles for a small boat, with other overlapping radial searches applied thereafter according to direction, current, wind, and drift.

Some ships have even sunk and then resurfaced at another place, as did the *A. Ernest Miles,* which sank with a cargo of salt off the Carolina coast. When the salt melted, the ghost ship came to the surface again, where it was subsequently found. Another ghost or derelict ship, the *La Dahama,* that rose from the deep sea is one frequently mentioned with reference to the Triangle as it was reported sunk in April 1935 and its passengers were rescued by the S.S. *Rex,* but sometime later the *Aztec* found her adrift off Bermuda. The crew of the *Aztec* did not know that the ship had previously been sunk and its passengers rescued and considered *La Dahama* to be a derelict mystery ship until the news came from the *Rex,* now back at its home port in Italy. *Why* the ship rose is still a mystery.

Wreckage of lost ships and planes on the sea floor, moreover, can easily vanish into ocean quicksands or can be covered up by storms, or eventually be uncovered by other storms, until rediscovered by submarines or divers. Mel Fisher, a longtime diver and salvor (one engaged in salvaging ships or cargoes), has been engaged for some years in underwater exploration on the continental shelf within the Triangle area in the Atlantic and Caribbean. While occupied in his search for Spanish gold, of which he has amassed a great quantity, he has made other surprising finds on the sea bottom which were evidently widely searched for at the time of their loss, but later forgotten. These metal concentrations are picked up by a magnetometer, a thousandfold intensity compass which indicates the location of undersea metal, a property that has often directed Fisher to relics other than the Spanish treasure ships he is usually searching for. (It is important to note that the improved magnetometer was not in use at the time of many of the disappearances within the Bermuda Triangle.) When divers descend to the ocean floor following the magnetometer's indications it often happens that, instead of Spanish galleons, they find lost fighter or private planes, various kinds of ships, and once, several miles offshore, a railway locomotive, which Fisher left on the bottom for marine archaeologists of the future.

Mel Fisher is of the opinion that some, among the many disappearances in the Florida-Bahamas area, have been caused by unexploded bombs from Air Force bomb runs, live torpedoes or floating mines from past wars or present combat training exercises. On one occasion, diving in the vicinity of a Spanish treasure ship, he started to bring to the surface what he thought was an antique Spanish cannon when he noticed that the barnacle-encrusted artifact had a pointed end, indicating that it was a bomb—and a live one!

From the number of unidentified wrecks he has noted on the bottom as he pursues his quest for the special wrecks he is seeking (two Spanish treasure galleons, *La Margarita* and *Santa María de Atocha,* containing treasure estimated as worth from $400,000,000 to $600,000,000), Fisher concludes that hundreds of ships have crashed on the reefs during storms and that many have been buried in the offshore sands. Even to reach some of the treasure ships he has already found it has been necessary, once metal has been indicated by the magnetometer, to excavate under the sea bottom in order to reach them. He observes that quicksands exist where the Gulf Stream flows past the end of Florida and these quicksands have been noted to swallow fairly large boats which became stuck in the sandy bottom.

Vagaries of currents and the shifting bottom might then be responsible for some of the unsuccessful searches for lost ships and planes. But there are other underwater features in the area which may also have been responsible for hiding the evidence of some of the disappearances.

These are the unusual "blue holes," scattered between the limestone cliffs and other underwater limestone formations throughout the Bahamas with the wide banks and abyssal drop-offs. Thousands of years ago these holes were limestone caves then above water, but when the waters rose as the result of the melting of the third glaciation—perhaps twelve to fifteen thousand years ago—the caves became the "blue holes," a favorite haunt of fish and, recently, of adventuresome scuba divers. These limestone caves and passageways go right to the edge of the continental shelf and some continue down through the whole limestone formation, to a depth of 1,500 feet, and others are connected through underwater passageways and caves with inland lakes and ponds on the larger Bahama islands. Although miles away from the sea, these smaller bodies of water raise and lower their levels with the tides of the ocean. Ocean fish, transported by underwater currents in this submarine system, suddenly appear miles inland. A twenty-foot shark made a sensational appearance in one of these quiet inland pools twenty miles from the shore, creating great agitation among the local inhabitants, accustomed to swimming in their peaceful pond.

The blue holes within the ocean are located at various distances from the surface. Divers entering these underwater holes notice that cave chambers branch off from the passages they are following exactly as is the case with cave formations on land. The passageways seem to go off in many directions, evidently confusing even the fish, which often swim upside down. Some of the passages between the caves seem to be so regularly formed that divers have looked for chisel marks to see if they were hand-cut at a time when the limestone cliffs were above sea level. Divers have noticed the dangerously strong currents flowing inside the blue holes. This is due to the tidal flow, which causes masses of water to enter the holes, creating a funnel effect with strong whirlpools on the surface, even though there is no land above water in the vicinity. Such a whirlpool could possibly drag a small boat down under water into a blue hole together with its crew. This possibility was given a certain credibility when the oceanographer Jim Thorne, on a diving expedition, found a fishing boat wedged deep within one of the blue holes at a depth of eighty feet. Dinghies and small craft have also been found by others, at sixty-five feet and lesser depths within the holes. But while some small boats and perhaps wreckage of larger boats may have ended up within the blue holes and may still be there, certainly this whirlpool effect would not explain the disappearance of ships and certainly not of planes.

Although whirlpools appear in various parts of the world's oceans at various times, and notably within the Bahamas area of the Bermuda Triangle, none of the known phenomena, except perhaps major seismic or atmospheric disturbances, could be compared with the oceanic whirlpool off Norway, described by Edgar Allan Poe in his "A Descent into the Maelström." Speaking of this ship-destroying whirlpool from a point on its vast inclined and revolving wall, the narrator says:

> . . . Never shall I forget the sensations of awe, horror, and admiration with which I gazed about me. The boat appeared to be hanging, as if by magic, midway down, upon the interior surface of a tunnel vast in circumference, prodigious in depth, and whose perfectly smooth sides might have been mistaken for ebony, but for the bewildering rapidity with which they spun around . . . As I felt the sickening sweep of the descent, I had instinctively tightened my hold . . . and closed my eyes. . . . Now looking about me upon the wide waste . . . on which we were thus borne, I perceived that our boat was not the only object in the embrace of the whirl. Both above and below us were visible fragments of vessels, large masses of building timber and trunks of trees, with many smaller articles, such as pieces of household furniture, broken boxes, barrels and staves. . . . I now began to watch, with a strange interest, the numerous things that floated in our company . . .
>
> "This fir tree," I found myself at one time saying, "will certainly be the next thing that takes the awful plunge and disappears,"—and then I was disappointed to find that the wreck of a Dutch merchant ship overtook it and went down before. . . .

Such writings may have influenced some of the theories concerning ships disappearing in the Triangle as well as the shape of "the gulfs [that] wash us down" at sea. A more likely doom for small and even larger boats in the area would be sudden tidal waves, or even waterspouts, the seagoing tornadoes which occur at certain seasons and which raise a vast funnel of water to a great height in the sky. A waterspout or several of them might well tear apart a small boat or a low-flying plane, in the same way that tornadoes on land tear apart or carry houses, fences, vehicles, and people into the sky. Moreover, while waterspouts can be seen during the day, when there is time to take evasive action, they are considerably more difficult to avoid at night, especially by a plane flying in low-visibility weather. But by far the greatest suspects, with regard to sudden sinking of ships, are unexpected tidal waves, usually resulting from underwater earthquakes. The creation of large waves depends on various factors: underwater earthquakes and landslides, atmospheric pressure, winds, storms, and hurricanes, not necessarily in the immediate area, or eruptions of undersea volcanoes. Huge waves can appear from a variety of causes in a calm sea, while waves in a rough sea have been estimated by competent observers to reach a height of at least 112 feet (U.S.S. *Ramapo,* February 6, 1963).

The huge waves caused by seismic disturbances (tsunamis) have been known to reach skyscraper heights of two hundred feet. These tsunamis can happen without warning and can easily sink a ship if the ship is anchored or capsize it if it is under way.

Not only do ships capsize when struck by these waves but sometimes even a large ship will break in half from the effects of tension, depending on how it is facing the waves and how far the troughs are apart between the waves. While smaller ships may ride over the crests of the waves and down into the troughs with-

Sketch of 200-foot-high waterspout as observed from shoreline. Waterspouts are sea tornadoes and are as dangerous at sea as a tornado is on land. The turbulence of a tornado can pull apart and scatter a small ship or plane coming into its direct path.

out difficulty, this fate overtook a destroyer, which was broken in two by great waves over which it extended a trough and a half, although it probably would have survived if its length had measured one *or* two of the temporary troughs.

There also exist other very destructive and unusual seiche waves, usually the product of underwater landslides caused by the pulling apart of a fault in the earth's crust. The seiche waves, smaller in height, are not as sensational-looking as the tsunamis, but they are immensely powerful, with great tides of water built up behind them. They are harder to recognize as they approach and they are therefore even more dangerous to ships. Such a wave, suddenly arriving without previous warning, could smash a ship and spread its wreckage over long distances, losing pieces of it as it traveled.

If ships can literally be swallowed by a sudden tremendous sea, is it equally possible for planes to disappear in the air? Planes have been seen by reliable observers to fly into a cloud but never fly out again— as if something had disintegrated them or snatched them out of the air during flight.

Stresses exist in the atmosphere that can be roughly compared with tidal waves, especially if a plane heads into them at a high rate of speed. Also, as there are often winds at different altitude levels, an ascending or descending plane can frequently encounter strong winds coming from a different direction than that indicated by the wind sock at the airport. If the intervening wind is strong enough, this can often have unfortunate results for the plane concerned. This "wind shear" factor is an important element in air losses and, in its intensified form of CAT (clear air turbulence) it can be compared to the seiche waves that unexpectedly occur in an otherwise calm sea. The turbulence may be going either up or down or in a different horizontal direction and, when the change is rapid enough, either through the force of CAT or the speed of the plane, the effect is almost like flying into a stone wall.

Generally speaking, CAT cannot be predicted, although it is generally encountered at the edge of the jet stream, the air current that moves through the skies above the earth much as the Gulf Stream moves through the ocean, but with considerably more speed—two hundred knots per hour as compared with the Gulf Stream's four knots or less. CAT could possibly explain the loss of some of the light planes in the Bermuda Triangle, tearing them apart according to the amount of pressure exerted (the G factor) or suddenly forming a vacuum and dropping the plane into the sea. CAT itself is a mystery, as it appears suddenly, if one can use the word "appear" for an invisible phenomenon, and it is unpredictable. Nevertheless, it is doubtful that sudden pressure change could have been the reason for all of the many planes lost in the Triangle and could have knocked out their radio communications as well.

Planes that disappear in the area in the future may be easier to find because of new sophisticated tracking and memory systems which, if they had been carried by many of the lost planes, might have enabled them to be found if they still existed. The aircraft of today also carry computerized memory systems called "AIDS"— Airborne Integrated Data Systems—which, if found, would preserve a record of what happened to the plane. It is now possible to audit and record at the base everything said in the cockpit of commercial and other aircraft. One remembers, however, that the conversations between the pilots on the planes of Flight 19 were heard at the base without shedding any light on what was happening. There are also systems in use, developed through the Mercury space flight and atomic submarines, which automatically record the position and any deviation of a plane or ship. A new device for locating a lost plane is called the "crash" or "recovery" beacon. It is a small radio transmitter, capable of transmitting for two or three days. It is located in the tail of the plane and is activated by the loss of the electronic system. But again, if disasters in the Triangle are connected with radio blackouts, one supposes that in such a case these new devices would also be neutralized.

Electromagnetism and the malfunction of instruments are recurring elements in the mystery of the Triangle. Hugh Auchincloss Brown, an electrical engineer and the author of *Cataclysms of the Earth,* is of the opinion that: "There are good reasons to connect these incidents to the magnetic field of the earth. There have been fearful reverses of the magnetic field at different periods of the earth's history and perhaps another age of a change in the magnetic situation is developing, with occasional magnetic 'earthquake' indications as prior warnings. This might explain the disturbances which would cause the planes to crash and then disappear, when they sank in deep water. But it would not account, of course, for the disappearance of the ships . . ."

Wilbert B. Smith, an electronics expert who headed a magnetism and gravity project for the Canadian Government in 1950, has suggested that these elements are a factor in plane disappearances. He stated that he had found specific locations, which he referred to as "areas of reduced binding," relatively small in area (about 1,000 feet in diameter but extending upward to a considerable height), which were in effect so turbulent that they could tear planes apart. Planes would therefore not have advance notice of these invisible and uncharted areas of magnetic and gravitational malfunction until they flew into them, with fatal effects. Smith wrote, in commenting on·the seeming impermanence of these locations:

> . . . We do not know if the regions of reduced binding move about or just fade away. . . . When we looked for several of them after three or four months we could find no trace of them. . . .

A spokesman for the Search and Rescue Branch, Coast Guard Headquarters, has also specified the importance of magnetism and gravity in the investigations:

> Quite frankly, we don't know what is happening in. this so-called Bermuda Triangle. All we can do about these unexplainable disappearances is speculate.
> The Navy is trying to get to the bottom of the mystery with a project called Project Magnetism in which they're investigating electromagnetic gravitation and atmospheric disturbances. Some experts think that some such disturbance might have disintegrated those planes in 1945. A ship in the area reported sighting a large ball of fire in the skies which, of course, could have also meant a midair collision—but that's an unlikely event among five planes. The fact is, we have no real opinions.

The Seventh Coast Guard District, the closest district to the Triangle, in a form letter previously referred to, takes the point of view that the Bermuda or Devil's

Triangle is an imaginary area (see page 53) and offers the comforting assurance that the many losses are simply a coincidence. The letter follows:

. . . The "Bermuda or Devil's Triangle" is an imaginary area located off the southeastern Atlantic coast of the United States, which is noted for a high incidence of unexplained losses of ships, small boats, and aircraft. The apexes of the triangle are generally accepted to be Bermuda, Miami, Fla., and San Juan, Puerto Rico.

In the past, extensive, but futile Coast Guard searches prompted by search and rescue cases such as the disappearances of an entire squadron of TBM Avengers shortly after take off from Fort Lauderdale, Fla., or the traceless sinking of the Marine Sulpher Queen in the Florida Straits have lent credence to the popular belief in the mystery and the supernatural qualities of the "Bermuda Triangle."

Countless theories attempting to explain the many disappearances have been offered throughout the history of the area. The most practical seem to be environmental and those citing human error.

The majority of disappearances can be attributed to the area's unique environmental features. First, the "Devil's Triangle" is one of the two places on earth that a magnetic compass does point towards true north. Normally it points toward magnetic north. The difference between the two is known as compass variation. The amount of variation changes by as much as 20 degrees as one circumnavigates the earth. If this compass variation or error is not compensated for, a navigator could find himself far off course and in deep trouble.

An area called the "Devil's Sea" by Japanese and Filipino seamen, located off the east coast of Japan, also exhibits the same magnetic characteristics. As the "Bermuda Triangle" it is known for its mysterious disappearances.

Another environmental factor is the character of the Gulf Stream. It is extremely swift and turbulent and can quickly erase any evidence of a disaster. The unpredictable Caribbean-Atlantic weather pattern also plays its role. Sudden local thunder storms and water spouts often spell disaster for pilots and mariners. And finally, the topography of the ocean floor varies from extensive shoals around the islands to some of the deepest marine trenches in the world. With the interaction of the strong currents over the many reefs, the topography is in a state of constant flux and development of new navigational hazards is swift.

Not to be under estimated is the human error factor. A large number of pleasure boats travel the waters between Florida's Gold Coast and the Bahamas. All too often, crossings are attempted with too small a boat, insufficient knowledge of the area's hazards, and a lack of good seamanship.

The Coast Guard, in short, is not impressed with supernatural explanations of disasters at sea. It has been our experience that the combined forces of nature and unpredictability of mankind outdo even the most far fetched science fiction many times each year. . . .

Almost as an afterthought the letter offers a brief bibliography, where the reader is referred to articles by Ivan Sanderson, Leslie Licher, Vincent Gaddis, and John Wallace Spencer, as a sort of "equal time" to those who believe that the mystery of the Bermuda Triangle is not so easily explained. In the last paragraph of the Coast Guard letter it is mentioned that:

. . . We know of no maps that delineate the boundaries of the Bermuda Triangle . . . [although it adds that] . . . among the Acromagnetic Charts of the U.S. Coastal Region, H.O. Series 17507 . . . Numbers 9 through 15 cover the "Bermuda Triangle."

Some civilian airline executives in the area are in cautious agreement with the Coast Guard opinion. Mrs. Athley Gamber, president of Red Aircraft in Fort Lauderdale, is one example. Athley Gamber, an attractive brunette, and a charming example of a vital, successful woman executive, is the widow of a pilot who disappeared on a flight between Fort Lauderdale and the Bahamas. She has been on the airfield during many search operations for missing planes and has had both motive and opportunity to speculate about the many private planes that have disappeared without trace within the Triangle.

Mrs. Gamber, from her observation point in the area, does not believe there is anything mysteriously sinister about the Bermuda Triangle. She is of the opinion that the reason that many pilots have not sent a Mayday or SOS was "that they had no idea that they were in trouble," adding that "the moment you get in worse condition, the radar is discontinued."

She observes: "This area is characterized by a rapid development of an almost spontaneous low. An aircraft is built for a certain shear load—after that it will come apart." She adds, "I am more convinced than ever that human nature cannot cope with the elements." She estimated that pilot error is responsible for as much as 50 per cent of the disappearances and that of the many private planes that have vanished, 25 per cent have simply run out of gas.

But the commercial, passenger, and military planes that disappear on normal runs with constant checking by experienced pilots and flight personnel certainly did not run out of gas, nor did the planes that vanished in groups all hit clear air disturbances at exactly the same time and at the same pressure, nor does there exist a believable explanation as to why nothing, in contrast with what happens in other parts of the world's oceans and shores, has ever been found from so many losses or why they vanished so abruptly from the sky. Again, what is applicable to aircraft is not applicable to ships, and if all of the air losses could be explained away, the ship losses in the Bermuda Triangle would remain as mysterious as ever. To the observer there appears to be an obvious correlation, at least in intensity, between the two types of losses, and each satisfactory explanation seems to bring with it one or several more questions—somewhat similar to the Hydra, a multi-headed monster of another, more ancient myth which, according to Greek legend, as soon as one head was cut off, was capable of growing another, a source of considerable dismay to its adversaries.

Widespread interest in the "mythos" of the Bermuda Triangle has increasingly preoccupied the imagination of dwellers on the adjoining shores as each new case is reported and discussed. Because of the frequent disappearances of small boats and planes, which could disappear from numerous other causes, there is no way to ascribe the disappearances to suspected forces in the Triangle, although they are generally associated with them in the public mind.

Robie Yonge, a leading Miami disk jockey and radio commentator, is an example of to what degree this mystery has intrigued observers in southern Florida.

Since he expressed his interest in the Bermuda Triangle, he has received literally thousands of calls, most of them while he was on the air, from listeners who have stories to tell or want more information. He is presently interested in the manning of a launch equipped with sending and control apparatus and with "bugged" dummies aboard, with the intention of setting it adrift between Florida and the Bahamas within the inner area of the Triangle and observing what happens to it through remote electronic control.

The desire to solve this mystery by personal search and involvement has extended much farther north. In the latter part of 1974, an organization bearing the name of the Isis Center for Research and Study of the Esoteric Arts and Sciences, of Silver Spring, Maryland, will conduct a "frontiers of science" seminar cruise, by chartered ship, of the areas of the Bermuda Triangle where the most unusual and potentially dangerous phenomena have been recorded. According to Isis president Jean Byrd, participants in the cruise will be required to take out special insurance because of the implied element of danger. In addition, it is planned to run psychological tests on members as they cruise through the "danger" areas, especially those where unusual compass activity, or lack of function, gives signs of magnetic deviation, to determine whether the mental states of the participants reflect the magnetic stress. This possibility has sometimes been previously mentioned as an explanation whereby persons mentally affected by strong magnetic currents would lose control of planes or ships, causing them to crash or founder or they would simply abandon ship under psychological stress. It must be pointed out, however, that the survivors who claim to have encountered the yet unidentifiable forces present in the Triangle do not remember noting any mental aberration except the understandable ones of surprise, fear, extreme concern, and future caution.

Lacking a logical and readily acceptable explanation, independent researchers concerned with the disappearances in the Bermuda Triangle have gone even farther afield—some to explanations based on exceptions to natural law, others to suggestions of interdimensional changeover through a passageway equivalent to a "hole in the sky" (which aircraft can enter but not leave), others believe the disappearances are engineered by entities from inner or outer space, while still others offer a theory or combinations of theories that the phenomenon may be essentially caused by still functioning man-made power complexes belonging to a science considerably older than and very different from ours.

6

Time-Space Warps and Other Worlds

INVESTIGATORS OF THE BERMUDA TRIANGLE HAVE long noted the existence of another mystery area in the world's oceans, southeast of Japan, between Japan and the Bonin Islands, specifically between Iwo Jima and Marcus Island, with a record and reputation indicative of special danger to ships and planes. Whether the ships have been lost from underwater volcanoes or sudden tidal waves, this area, often called the Devil's Sea, enjoys at least officially an even more sinister reputation than the Bermuda Triangle in that the Japanese authorities have proclaimed it a danger zone. This action came about after an investigation carried out by Japanese surface craft in 1955.

The Devil's Sea had long been dreaded by fishermen, who believed it was inhabited by devils, demons, and monsters which seized the ships of the unwary. Aircraft

and boats had disappeared in the area over a period
of many years, but during the time when Japan was at
peace, nine modern ships disappeared in the period of
1950 to 1954, with crews totaling several hundred
persons, in circumstances characteristic (extensive air-
sea searchers, lack of wreckage or oil slicks) of the
happenings in the Bermuda Triangle.

The Bermuda Triangle and the Devil's Sea share a
striking coincidence. The Bermuda Triangle includes,
almost at its western terminus, longitude 80° west, a
line where true north and magnetic north become
aligned with no compass variation to be calculated.
And this same 80° W changes its designation when it
passes the poles, becoming 150° E. From the North
Pole south, it continues on, passing east of Japan, and
crosses the middle of the Devil's Sea. At this point in
the center of the Devil's Sea, a compass needle will
also point to true north and magnetic north at the same
time, just as it does at the western border of the Bermuda Triangle on the other side of the world.

The unexplained losses in this Japanese equivalent of
the Bermuda Triangle were instrumental in inspiring
a government-sponsored investigation of the area, which
took place in 1955. This expedition, with scientists
taking data as their ship, the *Kaiyo Maru No. 5,* cruised
the Devil's Sea, ended on a rather spectacular note—
the survey ship suddenly vanished with its crew and
the investigating scientists!

The presence of one or more other areas of disappearance in the world's oceans has led to some
unusual speculations. Theories concerning antigravity
warps have been advanced, presupposing areas where
the laws of gravity and normal magnetic attraction no
longer function in ways with which we are familiar.

Ralph Barker, author of *Great Mysteries of the Air,* noting that new developments in physics point to the "evidence of the existence of anti-gravitational particles of matter" suggests that "the presence of anti-gravitational or 'contra-terrene' matter, of a nature completely contrary to those on this planet . . . of appalling explosive character when [it] comes into proximity of matter as we know it . . . embedded in localised areas of the earth . . ." He offers the possibility that this matter may have arrived from space and become embedded under the earth's crust, sometimes under the land but more often under the sea.

Consideration of this theory offers a possible explanation of electronic and magnetic malfunction within given areas but would not, however, explain the many losses of ships and planes within sight of land. One remembers, in this connection, reports of other areas of magnetic anomaly over other bodies of water throughout the world where the pull of something under the water is stronger than that of the North Magnetic Pole.

A more detailed study of the Bermuda Triangle and other suspect areas was made by Ivan Sanderson and discussed in his article "The Twelve Devil's Graveyards Around the World," written for *Saga* magazine. In plotting ship and plane disappearances throughout the world, Sanderson and his associates first found that the majority of these mysterious losses occurred in six areas, all of them having more or less the same lozenge shape and coincidentally located between latitudes 30° and 40° north and south of the Equator and including the Bermuda Triangle and the Devil's Sea.

Developing his theory further, Ivan Sanderson established a network of twelve "anomalies" at seventy-two-

degree intervals around the world, centered more precisely at 36° north and south latitude, making five in
the Northern Hemisphere, five in the Southern and including the North and South poles. The reason for the
Bermuda Triangle being the most celebrated, he suggests, is that it is the most traveled while the others,
although located in less traveled areas, also give considerable evidence of magnetic space-time anomalies.

The majority of these active areas lie due east of
continental land masses where warm ocean currents
going north collide with cold currents going south. In
addition to this current collision, these areas also represent the nodal points where the surface ocean currents
turn one way and the subsurface currents turn in another direction. The great subsurface tidal currents
sweeping tangentially, and influenced by different tem-
peratures, set up magnetic vortices, affecting radio
communication, magnetism—perhaps even gravity—
and eventually, in special conditions, causing air and
surface craft to vanish—sailing or flying off into a
different point in time and space. An interesting side-
light on the erratic behavior of these areas is under-
lined by Sanderson in describing the astonishing "early
arrivals" of carefully clocked-in air flights where planes
have arrived so far ahead of schedule that the only
possible explanation would be that they had a tail wind
behind them blowing, for example, at 500 miles per
hour. Such incidents may be the result of unrecorded
winds but they seem to occur most frequently within
the Bermuda Triangle and other vortex areas, as if these
particular planes had encountered the anomaly but had
skirted or been propelled safely through the "hole in
the sky" that had cost so many travelers their lives.

An incident involving time lapse occurred at the

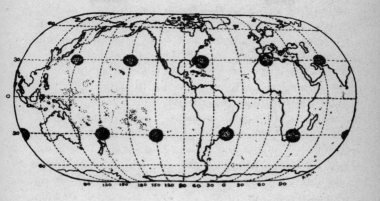

Twelve sections of the world, vortices of electromagnetic aberrations, as suggested by the theory of Ivan Sanderson. The two areas not shown on this projection are at the poles. The area to the east of Japan corresponds to the Devil's Sea, the Japanese equivalent of the Bermuda Triangle.

Miami airport about five years ago which has never been satisfactorily explained. It concerned a National Airlines 727 passenger plane which, on approach to landing from the northeast, and being tracked on radar by the Air Control Center, suddenly disappeared from the radar screen for about ten minutes and then reappeared. The plane landed without incident and the pilot and crew evinced some surprise over the expressed concern of the ground crew since, as far as the crew was concerned, nothing unusual had happened. By way of an explanation one of the Air Control staff said to one of the pilots, "Man, for ten minutes you just did not exist." It was at this point that the crew checked their watches and the various time indicators in the plane and discovered that they were uniformly ten minutes slow according to real time. This was especially remarkable as the plane had made a routine time check twenty minutes before the incident and at that time there was no time discrepancy.

Noting that our planet operates on electromagnetism, Ivan Sanderson poses a question as to whether the Bermuda Triangle and certain other areas, functioning as ". . . . vast machines, generate still another kind of anomaly . . . Could they create vortices in and out of which material objects can drop into or out of other space-time continua?" For besides the many disappearances that have taken place, a vastly greater number of appearances have occurred in recent years and over the centuries, throughout the world, and seem to continue to occur despite official denials and the fact that they are logically "impossible."

No investigator of events in the Bermuda Triangle can avoid confronting reports of UFOs (unidentified flying objects). UFOs have been the subject of thousands of reports and investigations in the United States since the first flurry of peacetime sightings in 1947, and throughout the world thousands of other sightings have been reported, ten thousand in 1966 alone. Many millions of people have allegedly seen UFOs in the United States and other countries. They have been reported and described by scientifically competent observers—in the words of Dr. J. Allen Hyneck, former Air Force consultant on UFOs, "The intelligence of the observers and reporters of UFOs is certainly at least average. In many cases above average. In some cases embarrassingly above average."

They have been photographed with varying degrees of clarity; they have been observed to accompany planes, occasionally interfering with and destroying them, and they have sometimes appeared in considerable numbers over such world capitals as Washington and Rome. United States Government, Air Force, and Navy releases have attributed most of the sightings to the moon, lunar halo, comets, mirages, balloons, bright stars, meteors, the planets (especially Venus), test aircraft, contrails, searchlights, the northern lights, fireballs, fireworks, autokinesis (when an object that is stared at seems to move), "after-mirage" (when an object that has been stared at fades so slowly from one's vision that it can still be seen elsewhere), will o' the wisps, hoaxes, or mass delusion. However, UFO reports continue to come in and several large UFO associations and the proliferation of books on the subject keep the question very much alive. Whatever they are, it seems certain that they are not secret weapons belonging to the powers of the earth. (Each side in World War II thought the luminous "foo fighters," which hovered around their fighting planes, to be secret weapons of their opponents.) Since, as has been trenchantly observed, *if* the UFOs were secret weapons the Russians could not keep silent through pride of invention, nor could the Americans, if they had invented them, keep it out of their own press. It is interesting to note that although the United States Air Force position remains that UFOs cannot be explained and therefore do not exist, Air Force regulation AFR 80-17 gave detailed instructions to pilots as to what steps to take when a UFO is sighted.

Many of the AFR 80-17 provisions are a credit to the investigative perspective of the Air Force as well as to the persistence of the UFOs, so often discredited in official reports.

The objectives as stated in the regulations are: ". . . to determine if the UFO is a possible threat to the United States and to use the scientific or technical data gained from study of UFO reports."

While the regulation reassuringly states: "The majority of the UFOs reported to the Air Force have been conventional or familiar objects which present no threat to our security"; it adds: "It is possible that foreign countries may develop flying vehicles of revolutionary configuration or propulsion." There is something of a paradox, however, in the statement that "frequently some alleged UFOs are determined to be aircraft"; closely followed by "except as aircraft are determined to be the stimulus for the UFO report, aircraft are not to be reported under the provisions of this regulation," since the viewer who might report an odd-looking object could not know whether it was an aircraft or not, especially as it would be operating in the air. The regulation further provides that: "Each commander of an Air Force base will provide a UFO investigative capability. When notice of a UFO sighting is received, an investigation will be implemented to determine the stimulus for the sighting."

The greater part of AFR 80-17 is concerned with the chain of command for reporting and investigating UFOs and instructions for processing the photographs taken of such objects. Included in the regulation, there are also instructions concerning information a base commander may impart to the local press when queried about UFOs seen in the area: "In response to local

Flight of TBM Avengers similar to the five planes of Flight 19 which vanished with a total of five officer pilots and nine crew members on December 5, 1945, while on a short routine training mission from Fort Lauderdale Naval Air Station after a series of radio messages indicating that their compasses and gyros were "going crazy," that everything looked wrong and strange and that the ocean did not "look as it should." No trace of the planes or crew was found despite an intensive air and sea search of 380,000 square miles of land and sea. *(PHOTO: National Archives)*

Closer view of Grumman Avenger bomber of the type that figured in the loss of Flight 19. The bombers were equipped with life rafts and were capable of a minute and a half flotation in case of crash landing in water. Crews were trained to abandon ship in sixty seconds. These factors, as well as the relative closeness of the incident to the base, make the complete disappearance of all five planes and crews all the more mysterious. *(PHOTO: Courtesy of Grumman Aircraft)*

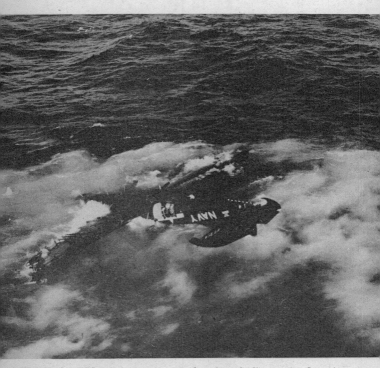

Crash of a TBM Avenger torpedo bomber similar to the five planes lost in Flight 19. While planes that crash into the sea usually leave an oil slick or some wreckage, the complete disappearance of Flight 19 elicited observations from the Naval Board of Inquiry such as: "They vanished completely as if they had flown to Mars." *(PHOTO: National Archives)*

A British vessel, also named the *Cyclops*, was lost in the North Atlantic during World War II. Again, a later examination of German submarine records showed no German subs to have been in the vicinity. *(PHOTO: National Archives)*

The *U.S.S. Cyclops*, lost on March 4, 1918. The unexplained disappearance of the *Cyclops* with 309 persons aboard has been classified as "one of the most baffling mysteries in the annals of the Navy." Following the theory that it may have been sunk by a German submarine, a postwar check of German sub operations revealed no German subs to have been in the area at the time. *(PHOTO: Official U.S. Navy Photo)*

Martin Mariner flying boat of the type similar to the plane sent to aid Flight 19. Shortly after takeoff on its search and rescue mission the Martin Mariner sent one message and then also disappeared with its crew of thirteen. *(PHOTO: National Archives)*

The *M.S. Marine Sulphur Queen*, a 425-foot freighter with a crew of thirty-nine. This large vessel disappeared in good weather on February 2, 1963, somewhere near the Dry Tortugas. No trace of the freighter or crew was ever found with the exception of a solitary life jacket found at sea fifteen miles south of Key West. *(PHOTO: National Archives)*

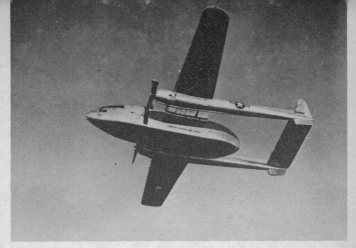

C-119 of type which disappeared with crew of ten in June 1965 within 100 miles of Grand Turk Island, Bahamas. At time of disappearance weather was clear and visibility good.

KC-135 Stratotanker, used for refueling. Two planes of this type were lost in August 1963, approximately 300 miles southwest of Bermuda. Since debris from the planes was found after an extensive search, it was presumed they had collided. But wreckage of the two planes was found at spots 160 miles distant one from the other. *(PHOTO: Courtesy the Boeing Company)*

Photograph taken from earth orbit looking south showing southern half of Florida, the Bahama Islands (Andros, Grand Bahama and Bimini), and part of Cuba. Dark area of sea shows the deep water between Florida and the Bahamas where many of the unexplained disappearances of planes and ships have taken place. Submerged Bahama Banks are shown as lighter ocean areas near islands. *(PHOTO: Courtesy National Aeronautics and Space Administration)*

Diver on edge of the Bahama Banks, an enormous submerged plateau of which the Bahama Islands are the crests. This huge underwater plateau is frequently honeycombed by limestone caves which sometimes connect with lakes in the interior of the present islands. (*PHOTO: Paul Tzimoulis, Courtesy* Skin Diver *Magazine*)

Scuba diver diving over edge of continental shelf in the Bahamas. While the sea bottom in large areas in the vicinity of the Bahamas is relatively shallow, the edge of the Bahama Banks drops sharply off to tremendous depths. *(PHOTO: Paul Tzimoulis, Courtesy* Skin Diver *Magazine)*

Interior view of a "blue hole," one of the underwater caves in the Bahama Banks. Strong currents sweep through these passageways and some small boats have been found wedged inside them. Stalactites and stalagmites within the "blue holes" indicate that they once existed above sea level for a considerable period of time. *(PHOTO: Paul Tzimoulis, Courtesy* Skin Diver *Magazine)*

The deep submersible *Aluminaut,* resting on the ocean bottom near Bimini in the Bahamas, has a design depth capacity of 15,000 feet. The fifty-one-foot aluminum-hulled vessel has taken part in research and salvage operations in many parts of the world. The *Aluminaut* can carry seven men, more than three tons of scientific equipment, stay submerged for up to three days, and has frequently worked more than a mile below sea level. *(PHOTO: Courtesy Reynolds Metals Company)*

The *Aluminaut* at work underwater. Its multiple uses include measurements of seismic and gravitational forces, speed and direction of subsurface currents, location of mineral deposits, salvage, and exploration and mapping of the ocean floor. *(PHOTO: Courtesy Reynolds Metals Company)*

Waterspout photographed on a clear day off North Bimini. Occasionally several spouts occur at the same time and while they are noticeable in daylight, they might not be seen by night-flying planes. *(PHOTO: J. M. Valentine)*

Moselle Reef, a location where many unidentified lights at night, visits by UFOs, and malfunction of equipment have been reported. The dark area at the top of the photograph is the drop-off to the abyssal deep. In this vicinity a sharp pinnacle rises a sheer 3,000 feet from the bottom but does not quite break the surface. *(PHOTO: J. M. Valentine)*

Aerial view of white waters as seen off Orange Key. The luminous white waters of the Bahamas and the Sargasso Sea have been a mystery ever since Columbus first observed them the night before his first landfall. The astronauts of *Apollo 12* also observed them, as the last lights visible from the earth. *(PHOTO: J. M. Valentine)*

Sister ship of the *Good News,* Captain Don Henry's 160-foot diesel-powered oceangoing tug reported to have engaged in a "tug of war" with unknown forces while pulling a barge in the Tongue of the Ocean. The *Good News* encountered unusual magnetic aberrations and electronic drain at the time of the incident, during which the barge temporarily disappeared within a thick haze. *(PHOTO: J. M. Valentine)*

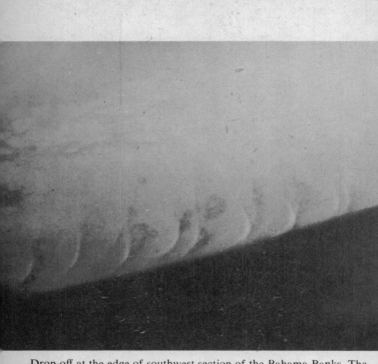

Drop-off at the edge of southwest section of the Bahama Banks. The area covered by this aerial photograph is all underwater. The land-like formations in the upper part of the picture are merely bottom features in shallow water towards the edge of the bank. The bank not only drops perpendicularly into the abyss but seems to curl slightly beneath itself as is evidenced by this photograph taken when conditions were unusually clear. *(PHOTO: J. M. Valentine)*

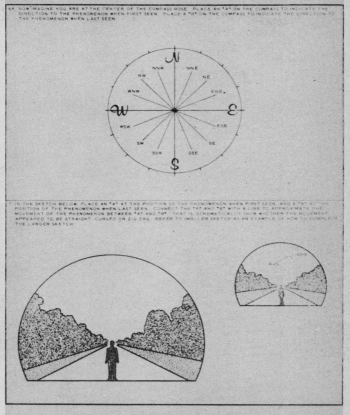

Attachment 1
(Becomes Attachment 1 to AFR 80-17)

1300

Illustration contained within (former) Air Force Regulation 80-17 with space indicated for viewer to fill in location and path of UFO he has allegedly seen.

The Buache Map of 1737, copied from ancient Greek maps, showing Antarctica without the ice. If the ice did not presently cover Antarctica, the Ross and Weddell seas would unite in a gigantic strait separating Antarctica into two land masses, a fact which was not established in modern times until the Geophysical Year of 1968. This map is another indication of surprising technological capabilities of some ancient cultures. *(PHOTO: Library of Congress)*

The Piri Reis map found in Istanbul in 1929, part of a world map said to have been recopied from a Greek original in the library of ancient Alexandria. Among other features, the Piri Reis map shows detailed features of Antarctica evidently drawn several thousand years before Antarctica was "discovered," as well as the true shape of Antarctica without the covering ice. Other features indicate an advanced knowledge of astronomy, trigonometry, and the ability to determine longitude, not known to our culture until the reign of George III of England. *(PHOTO: Library of Congress)*

Air view of Nasca Lines, Peru. These lines of unknown antiquity depict animals, birds, geometrical shapes, and, as considered by many, landing strips. Difficult to notice from the ground, they were not identified until the middle of the twentieth century—and then only from aerial surveys. The black line cutting diagonally through the landing strip is the Pan-American Highway. Astronauts of Skylab 2 were instructed to take pictures of the Nasca Lines with a view to determining whether they had some special significance when seen from space but space-photographing them has so far proved unsuccessful.

Maya stone carving from Palenque, Chiapas, Mexico, frequently cited by believers in prehistoric visits by ancient astronauts as a proof of such visits and their picturization by ancient Maya who observed them or were told about them. The Russian science writer Kazantsev considers the plaque to be the representation of a space vehicle complete with recognizable though stylized antenna, flight direction system, turbo compressor, control panel, tanks, combustion chamber, turbine, and exhaust.

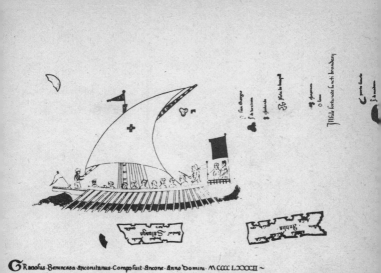

The Bennicasa Map of 1482, which Columbus may have had with him on his first voyage. The top of the map points east to the coasts of Spain and Portugal and some of the Atlantic islands shown were known to European seamen while others were legendary. Antilia, the island at the bottom right of the map, was reputed from Carthaginian times to be a large island in the western Atlantic. *(PHOTO: Library of Congress)*

The Great Pyramid of Gîza, Egypt, perhaps a surviving artifact of a previous world culture which existed at a time prior to dynastic Egypt. Measurements of different aspects of the Great Pyramid suggest that it served as a gigantic marker, an astronomical clock, and a mathematical and astronomical conservatory, preserving in stone the previously unsuspected knowledge held by "predawn" cultures. *(PHOTO: Courtesy Trans World Airlines)*

Cyclopean walls of fortress of Sacsahuaman, Peru, somewhat resemble the underwater constructions at Bimini. The walls at Sacsahuaman and other pre-Inca remains in Peru (seen here as partially filled in by subsequent Inca work with smaller stones) are themselves an archaeological mystery since they are of extreme age with the stones set so closely they seem fused. There is no explanation of how huge stones with odd exterior and interior angles could be transported, cut, measured, and set to exact but also random specifications by prehistoric people of whom even the Incas have no records. *(PHOTO: Courtesy Pan American World Airways)*

The Black Pagoda at Konarak, India, a surviving example of the surprising architectural capabilities of ancient times, especially the transportation of the enormous piece of stone covering the top of the tower. Technological advances of extremely ancient cultures in India suggest a link with even earlier cultures where science had progressed to awareness of heavier-than-air flight, rocketry, atomic structure, and a concept of the Earth and its place in the universe similar to that of today. *(PHOTO: Courtesy Government of India Tourist Office)*

A golden artifact from a pre-Columbian tomb which, despite its estimated age (1,800 years), is considered by many researchers to be a model of a prehistoric plane, complete with delta wings, engine housing, cockpit, windshield, a flanged tail, and elevators. A copy of this controversial object is on display in the permanent World of Man exhibit in Montreal. Similar golden objects, resembling planes, have been found in different locations in South America. *(PHOTO: Jack Ullrich)*

Diver investigating channel running between sections of Bimini Wall. Shape and placement of these monoliths, right-angle corners, and pillars underneath some of the stones are a conclusive, although not yet universally accepted, proof that they are man-made. *(PHOTO: J. M. Valentine)*

View of Bimini Wall showing passage or trench running down the middle of the construction, the regularity of this trench being still another indication that the structure is man-made. *(PHOTO: J. M. Valentine)*

lose-up of large monoliths comprising Bimini Wall. Other similar
ormations may be under the bottom sand, indicated only by un-
aturally straight lines of bottom growth patterns. *(PHOTO: J. M.
Valentine)*

erial photograph through water of sea bottom south of Bimini.
he great square shape in the right-hand corner is thought to be
e remains of a prehistoric dock or temple platform now under-
eath the bottom but affecting bottom vegetation which reflects its
ctilinear lines. *(PHOTO: J. M. Valentine)*

Stone frieze from Maya ruins at Cobá, showing stylized escape from a cataclysm marked by exploding volcanoes and, in the upper left corner, collapsing temple pyramids. Maya legends recount that the ancestors of the Mayas originally came from a great land in the

"Eastern Sea" which was overcome by a cataclysm and sank beneath the waves. Amerindian traditions refer to this land as Aztlán or Atlán and other similar names reminiscent of the sound of "Atlantis." *(PHOTO: J. M. Valentine)*

Air view of drop-off east of Cay Lobos, Bahamas. The dark water is the Old Bahama Channel, north of Cuba. The light-colored area in the right side of the photograph is also underwater but part of the Bahama Banks. The lines in the lower right-hand section indicate underwater remains which may have been part of a wall or road overlooking the sea millennia ago when the Bahama Banks were above water. *(PHOTO: J. M. Valentine)*

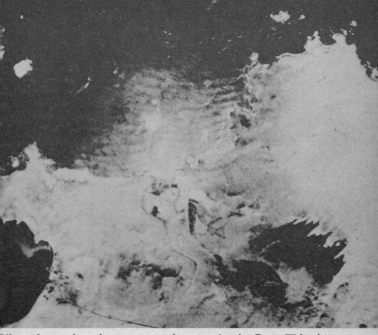

View of oceanic action on mountains near Ancón, Peru. This view, taken at an altitude of six miles, shows evidences of wave action on sides of mountain in lower-right of the photograph. The fingerlike projections still contain fossils of mollusks and other sea fauna. Along the coast of Peru, in this area, geological cross-bedding indicates that the former sea bottom, layers of which contain extremely ancient cultural vestiges, has been forced up out of the ocean.

Indications of deep land submergence in the Mediterranean. The diver is on the summit of a submerged acropolis 100 feet below the surface of the Aegean Sea near the island of Melos. While parts of the Mediterranean and other coastlines have sunk gradually over the centuries, some sections have evidently been precipitated suddenly to considerable depths. From the place where this photograph was taken, roads lead downward to constructions at even greater depths. *(PHOTO: Jim Thorne)*

Colossal water-worn limestone statue within the Loltún Caverns, Yucatán, Mexico, now several hundred feet above sea level. These enormous caverns, still incompletely explored, contain titanic statues of immense age, totally unrelated to other Amerindian culture patterns. Oceanic fauna embedded within the folds of these statues indicate that the statues, made above water, were submerged for a considerable period of time and perhaps resurfaced at the time that the Bahama Banks and other Atlantic islands sank below sea level. (PHOTO: J. M. Valentine)

The first photograph of the Bimini Wall taken from several feet above sea level, the clarity of the water permitting a clear view of the artifact at a depth of several fathoms. It is considered probable that this structure was not noticed previously since it was covered by the sea bottom but that storms or tectonic stresses may have occasioned its recent discovery in 1968. *(PHOTO: J. M. Valentine)*

inquiries regarding UFOs reported in the vicinity of an Air Force base, the base commander may release information to the news media or the public after the sighting has been positively identified. If the stimulus for the sighting is difficult to identify at the base level, the commander may state that the sighting is under investigation and conclusions will be released by SAF-OI afer the investigation is completed. The commander may also state that the Air Force will review and analyze the results of the investigation. Any further inquiries will be directed to SAF-OI." Translated into civilian idiom this might read: "If it is not a plane or something else you can explain, tell them to wait—and meantime don't get out on a limb."

Attachment 1 to the above regulation is, in effect, a checklist question worksheet of about half a dozen pages containing diagrams, questions, and suggested answers to assist exact and classified reporting of UFOs. Question No. 13, for example, requests the person reporting to check with a "yes," "no," or "unknown" one of several possibilities concerning the action of the alleged UFO he has seen. The questions are phrased as follows: "Did the phenomenon—move in a straight line?—stand still at any time?—suddenly speed up and run away?—break up in parts and explode?—change color?—give off smoke?—change brightness?—change shape?—flash or flicker?—disappear and reappear?—spin like a top?—make a noise?—flutter or wobble?" The question is interesting in that it reads like a résumé of what viewers have reported when they saw or thought they saw flying saucers, that is, everything except the little green men or other humanoids that some viewers have glimpsed inside.

The Air Force, perhaps the service most closely connected with UFOs, contracted with the University of Colorado to prepare a study and final report on UFOs which was duly produced in 1968. This project, under the direction of Dr. Edward A. Condon, scientific director of the final report, "Scientific Study of Unidentified Flying Objects," found, after a detailed study of a wide range of case histories, that most reports submitted were explainable one way or another and that only a small percentage could not be explained. It was also found that the amount of time and money spent researching UFOs did not justify the scientific information obtained, with the implication that any further effort would be wasteful. Meanwhile the UFOs continued to be sighted, singly and in massed flights, in the skies over different parts of the world and also in space.

Besides constant official denials, an obvious disadvantage to planned UFO research is the general nervous levity provoked by information media as they make reports to the public concerning UFO sightings. When reports of UFOs increased measurably in October 1973, being sighted in Louisiana, Ohio, Mississippi, Minnesota, Georgia, and Florida, and witnesses included such presumably level-headed persons as the governor of Minnesota and numerous police officers and state troopers, sufficient public interest was generated to warrant frequent reports by the press and networks. In this instance CBS radio offered its listeners a fairly detailed report of the sightings—but delivered it in rhyme! Another report informed the public that the Detroit police force had established a procedure for dealing with the occupants of UFOs when and if they should be taken into custody, even providing separation of sexes in the case of male and female captives (always providing that earthly biological differences may be in effect among the hundreds of millions of potentially inhabited planets).

The persistence of UFO reports and official non-recognition often elicits believers' feelings similar to those expressed by E. J. Ruppelt, who headed an Air Force investigation of UFOs, in his book *The Report on Unidentified Flying Objects:*

> What constitutes proof? Does a UFO have to land at the River Entrance to the Pentagon, near the Chiefs of Staff offices? Or is it a proof when a ground radar station detects a UFO, sends a jet to intercept it, the jet pilot sees it and locks on with his radar, only to have the UFO streak away at phenomenal speed? Is it proof when a jet pilot fires at a UFO, and sticks to his story even under threat of court-martial? . . .

Reports of UFOs in the southern Florida-Bahamas area have been and continue to be numerous out of all proportion to sightings elsewhere. They have been seen under the clear waters as well as in the skies, and going from the sky to the sea and from the sea to the sky, by numerous reliable observers. The number of locations of sightings have given rise to theories that the presence of UFOs has something to do with the disappearances in the Bermuda Triangle or rather, to be more explicit, that UFOs have been hijacking planes and ships for generations.

One of the most expressive supporters of the above theory is John Spencer, author of *Limbo of the Lost.* Spencer is familiar with aircraft, being a flyer himself and an Air Force veteran of ten years' service, and he is also a student of UFO phenomena and a member of NICAP (National Investigation Committee on Aerial Phenomena), a serious research organization for the study of UFOs which includes among its members top echelon United States Government, Navy, and Rocket personnel. Spencer became interested in the Bermuda Triangle, which he prefers to call the "Limbo of the Lost," during the time of the disappearance of the U.S. atomic submarine *Scorpion,* which many people connected at the time with other losses in the Bermuda Triangle. The loss of the *Scorpion* did not remain a mystery, however, as it was finally located over 400 miles from the Azores, partially through, in Spencer's opinion, previous Russian tracking obligingly made available to the U. S. Navy. He continued, nevertheless, to study the disappearance area and, projecting reported losses on a chart, concluded that almost all of them occurred on the continental shelf from Cape May, New Jersey, to the end of Florida and beyond, continuing east to the Gulf of Mexico and southwest to the Antilles, including also a 450-mile circumference of Bermuda and the whole Bahama Banks.

Spencer, who has studied the problem of the disappearances for many years, feels that the only believable explanation for the disappearance of planes and ships, complete with their crews and passengers, is that they have been and are being physically carried off from the seas or skies where they were traveling. He observes:

Since the complete disappearance of 575-foot vessels in calm seas 50 miles offshore or commercial airliners going in for a landing *cannot* happen according to earthly standards and yet *are* happening, I am forced to conclude that they are being taken away from our planet.

Examination of details of reported sightings of UFOs, not only in our own times, but throughout recorded history, have led him to believe that there exist two main types. One would be the ubiquitous "flying saucer" of about eighty-foot circumference, and the other, a tremendous mother ship able to carry a dozen or more "saucers" in its interior—or perhaps large specimen vessels from Earth. This gigantic spacecraft carrier would correspond to the sometimes reported huge oblong or cylinder-shaped (occasionally referred to as "cigar-shaped") objects sighted at various times, but not so often as the "flying saucers."

Spencer thinks that the reason so many "strikes" are made in the Limbo/Triangle is that the opportunities for taking human specimens there are more numerous, as in general the presumed raiders seem to avoid land operations and contact with human beings. The area is crowded with travelers by sea and air and it is easy for them (the alien entities) to get in and get out. The functional power of the UFOs may be, in his opinion, based on a sophisticated use of radio frequency as a propellant, which, in turn, would explain the electronic drain noted in most of the incidents.

Spencer's theory of why space kidnaping on such a scale would occur is an intriguing one and is shared by several other investigators who seem to have arrived at it independently of one another. Pointing out that among the staggering number of planets in the other solar systems within our galaxy (there are approximately 10^{21} stars, each presumably with its own solar system!), the law of averages presupposes the existence of highly developed civilizations, he suggests the possibility that the populations of other planets in the past have blown themselves up through misuse of energy and become flaming suns, leaving no vestige whatsoever of their history, populations, or scientific and cultural development. Therefore, visitors from other worlds may possibly either be interested in preserving a living relic of earth on some other planet or may wish to check the advancement of our present civilization on the earth before misuse of nuclear power becomes a danger to other planets. Or they may have other motives, of which we cannot possibly conceive.

Perhaps these alien intelligences are even willing to let us go our own way while they observe us, but are taking specimens they will preserve as an example of earth life as it was before the planet destroyed itself, which, in the case of other planets, they were perhaps not able to accomplish in time.

Examination of the many reports of what may have been UFOs *before* the age of the airplane gives one the impression that Earth has long been under observation from other worlds and other civilizations. However, since throughout history man has looked to the heavens for signs and portents (and almost always found them), it is sometimes difficult to differentiate between actual UFOs (if they so were) and the many fiery portents from the heavens to be variously interpreted as warnings, encouragements, or prophecies. An excerpt from the annals of Thutmose III, an Egyptian pharaoh of the XVIII dynasty, identified in the Egyptian Museum in the Vatican, may be the earliest written record of UFOs seen in antiquity. Contrary to some of the visionary accounts of later centuries, it describes the unusual apparition with commendable reportorial detachment:

In the year 22, the third month of winter, the sixth hour of the day, the scribes of the House of Life . . .

noted that a circle of fire was coming from the sky
. . . its body was 1 rod long and 1 rod wide . . .
they laid themselves on their bellies . . . [then] went
to Pharaoh to report it. His Majesty was meditating
on what was happening then . . . these things became
more numerous in the sky than before . . . they shone
more brightly than the shining sun and extended to
the limits of the four supports of heaven.

The army of Pharaoh looked on . . . with him in
their midst. It was after the evening meal that these
fire circles ascended higher in the sky to the south.

Pharaoh caused incense to be burned to reestablish
peace in the land and ordered what had happened
to be written in the annals of the House of Life . . .
so that it be remembered forever . . .

One notes that Pharaoh maintained his aplomb under
stress, befitting a god, as he was considered and perhaps
even considered himself, although somewhat mystified
by this manifestation from other, superior gods.

The Gilgamesh epic of ancient Babylon, probably
inherited from the preceding civilization of Sumeria,
describes the hero Etana's being taken aloft by the gods
over the earth until he is so far away from it that to
him the sea looked like a water trough and the land
looked like porridge, more or less what he would have
seen had he been observing the Red Sea, the Persian
Gulf, and nearby lands from a great (or orbital) height.

The fiery visitation seen by Ezekiel—"the whirlwind
out of the north . . . a fire enfolding itself . . . out of
the midst thereof came four living creatures . . ." has
frequently been cited as a UFO, one that landed and
subsequently took Ezekiel aboard as a passenger. This
heavenly vision, or perhaps spaceship, took place in the
seventh century B.C. and is the subject of much of the

Book of Ezekiel in the Bible. It has recently been the subject of investigation in an unusual German book *Da Tat Sich Der Himmel Auf* (*The Heavens Were Opened*), and recently published in English as *The Space Ships of Ezekiel*. It was written by Josef Blumrich, a rocket engineer and designer now on duty with NASA in Huntsville, Alabama.

Dr. Blumrich began his book with the intention of debunking the sometimes expressed theory that Ezekiel's vision was actually a spacecraft. As he researched his subject, however, and noted that Ezekiel's detailed references to the apparition he had seen made perfect sense if the "wheels within wheels" were applied to helicopter power which would enable the main rocket vehicle to hover over the land, and that the usual phenomena of rocket landing and takeoff were clearly and matter-of-factly described by Ezekiel, both to the changing colors according to speed, the blast of wind, the landing gear, and even the asbestos-resembling dress of the occupant, Dr. Blumrich then reversed his standpoint. He thereupon wrote a book diametrically opposed to the one he had started, establishing through biblical reference not only that Ezekiel had repeatedly seen a spacecraft but also that the being described by Ezekiel as the Lord was simply the captain of the rocket!

Ezekiel's narrative is but one of a long series of historical reports of what may have been UFOs of antiquity and the Middle Ages, the Renaissance, and early modern times. The different ways that viewers have described them through the centuries are fanciful, varied, and often amusing. But their very variety may furnish a thread of corroborative reporting when we consider that those who saw them described them with the vocabulary which came most naturally to their be-mused minds. We may suppose that Ezekiel, for ex-ample, used terms like "lion," "ox," and "eagle" to describe features of the rocket, and likened what may have been part of the landing gear to a calf's foot (a rather apt description) since he, belonging to a pastoral economy, was familiar with these domestic and wild animals.

Alexander the Great and his army, being, for their part, eminently familiar with warfare, likened to "great shining silvery shields" an apparent UFO foray of 329 B.C. which interfered with the passage of the Greek army as it was advancing over the Jaxartes River into India. Aristotle (384–322 B.C.), being familiar with the thrown discus of the Greek athletes, qualified the objects he saw in the sky as heavenly disks. The more bellicose Romans saw them, like Alexander, as shields or fiery darts or fleets of ships. Pliny, in Volume II of his *Natural History* (100 B.C.), wrote: "In the con-sulship of Lucius Valerius and Gaius Valerius a burn-ing shield scattering sparks ran across the sky at sunset from east to west." The Hawaiians describe the objects they have been seeing for a reported thousand years as *"akuatele"*—flying spirits. In the religious Middle Ages, in Europe, the moving objects seen in the night skies seemed to be crosses. (Could the history-changing cross seen by Constantine have been one of these?) And sometimes, as in Ezekiel, they were described as burn-ing and revolving wheels.

In the age of discovery and exploration the heavenly travelers assumed, to the eyes of the viewers, the like-ness of ships, and still later, after balloons had been invented, the flying objects were described in France as "shining fiery balloons." In nineteenth-century Vermont, the weaving-oriented observers called what they saw "an aerial spindle."

While observers from each successive period tended to name the moving objects in the sky by names which came most readily to their lips in moments of stress, it remained for our own culture to call them at first "flying saucers" or "cigar-shaped objects." As a matter of interest, at the time of the first two-day mass sightings in the United States in 1947, first over Iowa and then over Mount Rainier in Washington, the UFOs were first called "disks" and subsequently "pie pans" before being called "saucers."

Frank Edwards, a longtime observer of unexplained phenomena, thinks that the tremendous blast in Siberia on June 30, 1908, in a deserted area along the Yenisei River near Lake Baikal (only reindeer were victims), although long considered to be the result of a meteorite striking the earth, was really an atomic blast caused by the explosion of a spaceship. He cites the Russian science writer Alexander Katzenev as stating that the damage, under recent investigation, is identical to that produced by man-made atomic blasts under similar conditions, with lingering radioactivity and fusing of metals. No meteoric fragments, although, of course, they might be much deeper within the earth, have been recovered. Edwards concludes: "In the catastrophe along the Yenisei River in 1908 we lost a guest from the universe."

M. K. Jessup, a writer on UFOs of considerable scientific and disciplinary preparation, being an astronomer and a specialized selenographer (expert on the moon), was of the opinion in his book, *The Case for the UFO's,* that the famous ship disappearances or mysteries within the Bermuda Triangle, including the

Freya, the *Mary Celeste,* the *Ellen Austin,* and many others, were caused by UFO activity. He goes farther afield than the Triangle, describing the disappearance of the entire crew from the *Seabird,* a large sailing vessel, who vanished *after* hailing a fishing vessel near their home port of Newport, Rhode Island, in 1850, with a log entry made two miles from port and with a prepared and undisturbed meal on the mess table. The *Seabird* apparently continued without the crew on her homeward way and beached herself high on the beach—"as if lifted by giant hands"—and then, although firmly stuck in the sand, vanished at night in a storm. From examination of these ship incidents, Jessup concluded that such disappearances were "almost impossible to explain except as *upward* . . . Something operating from above, with great and decisive power, and suddenness of action . . ." He comments on a suggestion of "selective ruthlessness . . . something of evasion or secretiveness . . ." adding, "All are attributes of intelligence."

Jessup was of the opinion that the development of our air age "is of great interest to our space neighbors" and that this may be the explanation of the increasing number of UFO sightings in recent years, concentrated to a notable extent in the Triangle area off the coast of Florida and around Cape Kennedy. On one occasion at Cape Kennedy on January 10, 1964, a UFO is reported to have zipped into the tracking range during the firing of a Polaris missile and for fourteen minutes the radar followed the erratic course of the UFO before getting back on the target missile. Though widely commented on by those present at the time, this report did not appear in the press—possibly because mysteries are not conducive to public confidence. Jessup's theory of UFO "interest" in our air age—which has, since his death in 1959, escalated into the space age—has been considerably strengthened by quite recent developments. UFOs have been observed during some of the space shots, notably Gemini 4 and 7. In Gemini 4, astronauts McDivitt and Borman observed a "bogey" progressing parallel with their craft and thought, for a time, that it might be necessary to take evasive action. Another "bogey" was reported as having followed Gemini 7. The Apollo 12 moon flight was, for a time, at 132,000 miles out in space, "escorted" by UFOs, one in front and one following. Their presence solicited from astronaut Gordon the observation that they were "very bright and seemed to be flashing at us" and later, in communication with the Houston Command Center, he said, "We'll assume it's friendly, anyway." Although there has since been no confirmation from the Houston Command Center or from NASA, these lights were also noted by observatories in Europe. Still later, on the same flight, another bright light, described by the astronauts as being "as big as Venus," was visible by the astronauts between them and the earth for about ten minutes and then disappeared.

While taking into account that UFOs may be anything unidentified, including parts of booster rockets and other debris in space, the activities of such UFOs, as well as their capacity for appearing and disappearing, seem to indicate an independent and non-orbital direction.

Concerning sightings of alleged UFOs in space flight by astronauts, Dr. Franklin Roach has observed in the *Condon Report* that the "conditions under which the astronauts made their observations are similar to those which would be encountered by one or two persons in the front seat of a small car having no side or rear windows and a partially covered, very smudged wind-shield"—an observation which, carried to its logical conclusion, would infer that nothing the astronauts might note through visual observation could be truly credited.

As has been the case with several other investigators of UFOs and happenings within the Triangle, Jessup became convinced that a covert censorship was smothering many important reports and developments. His last book before his death was about biblical reports of "flying saucers," and he was also preoccupied with the question of how controlled magnetism could produce invisibility, an outgrowth of Einstein's "unified field theory," which Jessup considered the key both to the sudden appearance and disappearance of UFOs and the disappearance of ships and planes. He was in Miami when he met his death on April 29, 1959. According to Dr. Manson Valentine, a longtime friend and one of the last persons who ever talked to him, Jessup was in a depressed state of mind. Dr. Valentine had invited him to dinner on the evening of April 20. Jessup accepted the invitation but never arrived. He died in his parked station wagon in Dade County Park of carbon monoxide poisoning, the exhaust pipe having been connected by a hose to the interior of the car. Probably because of Jessup's insistence on certain aspects of intervention in the affairs of this world from other worlds, there are those who consider that Jessup's death was *not* self-induced and that the incident is an indication of the dangers of too close research in this field.

Dr. Manson Valentine, a zoologist, archaeologist, and oceanographer, has studied for several decades the unusual happenings in the Bermuda Triangle from the Triangle itself—Miami, the Bahamas, and other islands.

As an *in situ* investigator he is an excellent source for ascertaining what has happened there in the past as well as what is happening now. Much of the information he has at his disposal, especially that which he recalls from his last conversations with Jessup, is so startling that it should be reported in Dr. Valentine's own words as expressed in the answers to the following questions:

QUESTION: *How long have you been involved in observing the Bermuda Triangle phenomena?*

For more than twenty-eight years, since the disappearance of the PBMs in 1945, I have collected data on disappearances, interviewed survivors of incidents, and kept notes of reports of UFOs in the area at the times of the disappearances.

Is there a notable increase of UFO sightings in the area at the present time?

There are more sightings in this area than at any other place. There have been many recent sightings of aircraft that we know are not planes and undersea craft that we know are not regular submarines.

A recent sighting of this latter variety was made by Captain Dan Delmonico in April 1973. He is a lifelong sailor and a calm observer of excellent reputation. He made two almost identical sightings of an unidentifiable object under the very clear water of the Gulf Stream—both in approximately the same area—about one third of the distance in navigation between Great Isaac Light, north of Bimini, and Miami, where the Gulf Stream waters are very deep. Both sightings were made at about four o'clock in the afternoon, with smooth seas and normal ground swell and excellent visibility.

In the case of both sightings a gray-white object, smooth and shaped, as he said, "like a fat cigar with rounded ends," rushed past the bow of his boat under water. Delmonico estimated the size of the object to be 150 to 200 feet long and its speed to be *at least* sixty to seventy miles per hour. When Delmonico suddenly caught sight of the underwater moving object, it appeared to be on a collision course with his boat and seemed to be getting ready to break surface just in front of him. Apparently sensing his presence, the object dived and vanished after passing directly under his craft. There was no turbulence and no visible wake. There were no elevators, fins or any other projections to interrupt the smooth surface, and no portholes.

UFOs in the sky have been seen so often in the Triangle by pilots of aircraft and crews of ships that they have become fairly commonplace, especially over the Tongue of the Ocean. What is more intriguing is the presence of hovering UFOs seen by rangers as well as by myself over the treetops in the Oke-fenokee Swamp. In central Florida I saw one with a blue beam pointing at the waters of a lake. Perhaps they were taking on water, or even samples of local fauna for study. At the time of the April 1973 black-out in southern Florida, blue-green lights and blue trailing lights were seen in the sky especially at Turkey Point—where the atomic reactor is. In the great blackout incident of the Eastern Seaboard some years back, a flight of about a dozen UFOs had been seen.

Do you have a theory on how UFOs are powered?

There are several possible theories. One method, useful only in our atmosphere, would be the possibility of a disk-shaped ship having a perimeter of cathode ray generators which could rapidly travel in any direction simply by operating the generators on the lead edge or side of desired motion. Then the

Sketches of two of the fourteen UFOs sighted by Dr. Valentine. The sighting on the left was made at midnight, August 21, 1963, near Ashton, south of Orlando, Florida. The object was apparently taking on water from a lake. The distance from the observer was estimated at about seventy-five yards. The UFO on the right was sighted above trees at the roadside on U.S. Route 441, a few miles south of Pearson, Georgia, at the edge of the Okefenokee Swamp, at 3 A.M. It appeared to be luminescent and was pulsating with a bluish light. Distance from observer, approximately 100 feet.

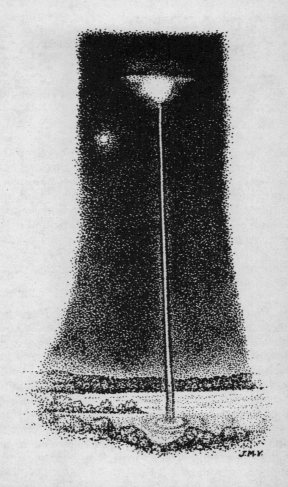

J.M.V.

UFO observed by Dr. Valentine at 2 A.M. on December 6, 1952, between Douglas and Fargo, Georgia. In Dr. Valentine's opinion the dark-core tunnel-like vortex shows what may be a stream of neutron emission indicating atomic fusion rather than a fission reaction, a possible non-polluting method of converting atoms into power. Such fusion would build up a magnetic field which would power the UFO at incredible speeds and possibly bring into the same field other moving objects in the immediate vicinity.

generators would ionize the air in front of the vehicle, thus causing a vacuum into which the craft could move. Pockets of ionized air left by UFOs quite possibly could be a cause of the clear air turbulence experienced by pilots.

Another method of propulsion would be similar to jet propulsion but infinitely faster and theoretically approaching the speed of light. The power reactors would concern atomic fusion rather than atomic fission. All that is required is fusionable material and water. This could account for UFOs being seen "lifting" water from inland lakes.

Still another theory involves the change of dimension and time warp based on special electromagnetic fields.

Did Dr. Jessup think there was a connection between the UFOs and the Bermuda Triangle?

He had a theory that the power of magnetic fields could transform and transport matter from one dimension to another . . . That UFOs could come into our dimension and get out again taking human or other samples with them. He further thought that some of the accidents were caused by the UFOs' cathode rays creating a vacuum which disintegrated planes when they entered this field. This is probably what happened to Mantel. [Note: On January 7, 1948, Captain Thomas Mantel and several other pilots at Godman Field, Fort Knox, took their P-51 Mustangs up after a UFO "of tremendous size" observed during daytime and approaching the base. When Mantel climbed after it, his plane was seen by witnesses to disintegrate. A later Air Force statement declared that the captain "blacked out while pursuing the planet Venus and that the plane fell apart in the subsequent dive."] He flew too close to the saucer, into the saucer's field of ionization. His plane exploded into so many pieces that nothing larger than the size of a fist was found. All pieces located were perforated as if little worms had bored through them.

This may have happened as well to the Constellation that Bob Brush [a commercial plane captain] saw explode near Great Inagua, in the Bahamas, back in October 1971. Bob was flying a DC-6 and got the Constellation on radar, flying low and possibly in trouble. Suddenly it exploded with a flare that lit the sky from horizon to horizon. The explosion was so brilliant that it hurt the eyes—absolutely unusual. A boat near the scene picked up a flight manual that Bob later examined and it was riddled with small holes, just like the bits of wreckage from Mantel's plane.

The UFOs, whatever they are, seem to create a temporary magnetic vortex, an ionization pattern that can cause ships and planes to disintegrate or disappear.

Jessup, before he died, believed that he was on the verge of discovering the scientific basis for whatever was happening, which he considered explainable according to Einstein's "unified field theory."

Can you give a simplified explanation of the unified field theory?

The basis of it is that all our compartmentalized concepts of time-space and matter-energy are not separate entities but are transmutable under the same conditions of electromagnetic disturbance. Actually the unified field theory offers yet another explanation of how UFOs could materialize and disappear so suddenly.

In practice it concerns electric and magnetic fields as follows: An electric field created in a coil induces a magnetic field at right angles to the first, each of these fields represents one plane of space. But since there are three planes of space, there must be a third field, perhaps a gravitational one. By hooking up electromagnetic generators so as to produce a magnetic pulse, it might be possible to produce this third field through the principle of resonance. Jessup told me that he thought that the U.S. Navy had inadvertently stumbled on this in a wartime experiment carried out on a destroyer which has been called the Philadelphia Experiment.

What was the Philadelphia Experiment?

According to Jessup the Philadelphia Experiment was a secret experiment conducted by the U. S. Navy in 1943 at Philadelphia and at sea. Its purpose was to test out the effect of a strong magnetic field on a manned surface craft. This was to be accomplished by means of magnetic generators (degaussers). Both pulsating and non-pulsating generators were operated to create a tremendous magnetic field on and around a docked vessel. The results were as astonishing as they were important, although with unfortunate aftereffects on the crew. When the experiment first began to take effect, a hazy green light became evident, something like the reports we have from survivors of incidents in the Triangle who tell of a luminous greenish mist. Soon the whole ship was full of this green haze and the craft, together with its personnel, began disappearing from sight of those on the dock until only its waterline was visible. The destroyer was subsequently reported to have appeared and disappeared at Norfolk, Virginia, which may have been the result of a trial invisibility run, involving a related time-warp phenomenon.

It was reported by a former crew member that the experiment was successful at sea, with an effective field of invisibility of spheroid shape extending one hundred yards from each beam, which showed the depression made by the ship in the water, but not the ship itself. As the force field intensified, some crew members began disappearing and had to be rediscovered by tactual contact and restored to visibility by a sort of laying-on-of-hands technique. Certain others became so far removed from their original material dimensions that they could only be detected and brought back to normalcy by a specially designed electronic device. For such cases, when a shipmate could neither be seen nor felt, the crew had a quaint expression: Being "stuck in molasses." Actually it was a state of suspended animation from which full recovery could be a serious problem. It was rumored that many were hospitalized, some died, others were adversely affected mentally. Psychic ability seemed to have been generally sharpened, while many retained the effects of transmutation from the experiment, temporarily disappearing and reappearing, either at home, walking on the street, or sitting in bars or restaurants, to the consternation of onlookers and waitresses. Twice the ship's binnacle suddenly burst into flames while being taken ashore, with disastrous results to the carrier.

Did Jessup witness these incidents?

I don't know how much he personally witnessed of the things he told me but he researched it pretty thoroughly. You must remember that he was not a "crank" writer but a distinguished and famous scientist and astronomer. He had been in charge of the largest refracting telescope in the Southern Hemisphere, directed several eclipse projects, was the discoverer of double stars, and had a brilliant scientific record. The reason that he became involved with the Philadelphia Experiment was that a man who claimed to have been a survivor of the experiment, named Carlos Allende (or Carl Allen), wrote to Jessup in 1956 about his book *The Case for the UFO's* because of the similarity of basic theory. Allende started a correspondence with Jessup, who naturally answered like any author answering fan mail. Some time after this correspondence began, Jessup was requested to come to Washington by the ONR (Office of Naval Research). Remember that censorship had covered up the Philadelphia Experiment except for one brief article in a Philadelphia newspaper. Jessup was shown a hand-annotated copy of his book which had mysteriously appeared in the Office of Naval Research with voluminous annotations referring to his theories, the Experiment, and

UFO activity. Jessup was asked if he recognized the handwriting apparently written by three different people, each of whom had identified the separate entries with his initials. He thought he recognized one script and the accompanying signature as those of Allende and submitted Allende's letters to the ONR. The Department of the Navy subsequently ordered to be reproduced, by an outfit in Texas, I think, twenty-five exact copies of the marked-up book with the notes printed in red. Jessup, who received three copies, was told that this was for top echelon circulation within the department. The Navy never officially admitted anything about the Experiment but they certainly were interested in the book. Jessup also told me that the Navy had tried to track down Allende from the return address on his correspondence but had failed, nor were the other commentators who had written on Jessup's book ever identified.

Why did Jessup kill himself?

If he committed suicide, it was probably due to extreme depression. He had been approached by the Navy to continue working on the Philadelphia Experiment or similar projects but had declined—he was worried about its dangerous ramifications. He was also despondent over the criticism directed against his books by the scientific and academic world.

You said, "If he committed suicide." Is there reason to believe that he was killed?

There were some comments—some people have thought so—perhaps he could have been saved. He was still alive when he was found. . . . perhaps he was allowed to die. His theories were very advanced and perhaps there were people or influences that wished to prevent their spread. It is curious that Jessup's own edition of the annotated navy book as well as a copy he had given to Briant Reeves [another writer on UFOs] disappeared from the mail when they were sent to other people.

Do you agree with Jessup's theories?

In general, yes. The whole question of magnetism is still largely a mystery. If we develop Einstein's implications in his unified field theory, which brought gravitational and electromagnetic fields within the theory of space-time, magnetic fields, if strong enough, would be able to cause objects and people effectively to change dimensions, thereby becoming invisible. The answer to the question of the Bermuda Triangle may perhaps be found in electromagnetic aberrations or *controls* that are evident only at certain times, when they are activated either by chance or by design, and it seems plausible that the presence of UFOs could create the necessary energy charges.

Why do you think there is such a concentration of incidents in the Triangle?

I believe it is possible that the intelligent beings which direct the UFOs are not only taking samples, checking our scientific progress, as evinced by their interest in Cape Kennedy and our space probes, but are returning to what may have been the location of ancient sacred sites, perhaps energy centers or power stations that are now covered by the sea. We have in recent years discovered, near Bimini and other places in the Bahamas, great building complexes on the sea bottom, an indication that a high state of civilization existed here many thousands of years ago. It is more than curious that so many incidents happen in this area and so many UFOs are seen not only in the sky but entering and leaving the ocean.

What can we do about UFOs and their implied menace?

There's really nothing we can do about it at the present time. I don't think there is much danger to most travelers and perhaps the people who have disappeared may still be alive, in another place or dimension. I think, however, that it is important to recognize the situation and to try to enter into some form of communication with them—that is what many of us are trying to do.

In light of what they obviously could do, we should consider ourselves fortunate that their activities have been so far largely benevolent, although there is always the possibility that these visitors do not come from the same places in outer or inner space, and do not share the same possibly "conservationist" views about our planet and its inhabitants.

If spacecraft either willfully or inadvertently are responsible for our major blackouts, it is a remarkable fact that not a single accident involving personal injury has been attributed to power shortage during these periods.

It is to be noted that both the great power blackout in the Northeast in 1965 and the Miami power failure of 1973 were followed by local reports of UFOs. During the Northeast blackout, sightings of a red shining ball 100 feet in diameter were made in Syracuse by observers who included the deputy commissioner of the Federal Aviation Agency. Other UFOs were sighted over New York, Newark, and Philadelphia, and numerous places in Massachusetts, Rhode Island, and New York State. A curious side effect, the malfunction of automobile motors in the vicinity of reported UFOs, has a bearing on the electrical drain and radio failure associated with their presence and reported by so many pilots of planes and ships in the Bermuda Triangle area.

It is evident, however, that many individuals, pre-judging the blackout situation in favor of the explanation that the presence of UFOs creates disturbances in the earth's magnetic field and electric communications and installations, were more on the lookout for celestial visitors at these specific times, especially since there were no interfering lights and the opportunity for examining the heavens was at an optimum.

In all events, while the site of the circuit breaker which caused the Great Blackout of 1965 has been indicated (the Sir Adam Beck No. 2 on the Niagara River), the initial cause has not been explained and an assessment made after the investigation is still essentially true: "The blackout caused by the failure of the northeast power grid created one of the biggest mysteries in the history of modern civilization."

Several of the most persistent observers of the Bermuda Triangle agree that if there is no earthly explanation for the disappearance of so many craft, then the explanation may well be an unearthly one—removal of ships, planes, and people through the agency of UFOs. In addition, the majority of UFO sightings are reported as lights of different colors and intensity noted at night, and some of the spectacular plane disappearances have been characterized by unusual lights reported in the night sky. This happened at the time of the Flight 19 incident and again in the case of the *Star Ariel*. However, although there is some agreement regarding UFOs and plane and ship disappearances, there is no agreement about where these UFOs may be coming from.

Somewhere in outer space, with its billions of possibly inhabited planets, would seem to be a plausible source of visits except that travel time, calculated in light-years, would take a good part of a lifetime, or many lifetimes. (The trip to the very nearest star—our own sun—would take only eight minutes by light-time, although the *next* nearest star, Alpha Centauri, is 4.3 light-years away.) But perhaps the length of a lifetime as we know it would be considerably different from that known on the planets of distant stars. Besides, new theories have arisen in recent years concerning the limit of speed—the speed of light, the curvature of space, and the relation of time to mass and energy which may eventually modify our concept of the time necessary for travel to other galaxies.

Some theorists suggest that the source of the visits may be nearer Earth, perhaps from the oceans of Earth itself. Ivan Sanderson, in his book *Invisible Residents,* pointing out that nearly three quarters of the earth lies under water (170,000,000 square miles of water to 60,000,000 square miles of land) and the fact that air breathers, living on the land bottom of the "air ocean," live fairly close to the surface of the earth, while water breathers, not limited to staying on the bottom of the hydrosphere, have a tremendously larger cubic volume in which to operate and develop, suggests the possibility:

. . . that there is an underwater "civilization" (or civilizations) on this planet that has been here for a very long time and which was evolved here, and/or that there are intelligent entities who have been coming here from elsewhere . . . which prefer to use the bottom of the hydrosphere, and possibly also the surface layers of the lithosphere below that, on or in which to reside and from which to operate.

He observes that, if such a civilization developed under water, it might be considerably further advanced than the surface civilization developed by the forms of life that left the sea for the land so many billions of years ago, inasmuch as remaining in the sea it would have had a head start in its original environment and continued to develop throughout the ages while concerning itself very little with events on dry land.

The presence of such developed entities and technological activities under the seas of the world may have given rise to the many sea legends recorded throughout history and even today, when unusual occurrences are noted and recorded with infinitely more precision than in previous times. This would explain the air-to-sea UFOs seen in the Bermuda Triangle as well as particular UFO interest in technical developments in Florida and over the adjacent waters. As for discovering the truth about their existence, it may be a question not so much of us discovering them as their discovering us and seeing in us a source of danger to their own environment.

Then there is the suggestion that UFOs fly in from another dimension and spirit planes, ships, and people out of ours. The theory of other coexistent dimensions, which touches on the theory of negative matter, a negative earth, and coexistent worlds, is somewhat less fanciful now than when it was first proposed several decades ago.

A famous explorer and aviator, Admiral Richard Byrd, who undertook flights over the intensified magnetic fields of both the North and South poles, made an incredible broadcast in 1929, while on a flight over the South Pole. He told of emerging through a foggy light into an area of a green land with ice-free lakes and reported seeing huge bisonlike beasts and other animals and what looked like primitive men. The broadcast immediately went off the air and Admiral Byrd's report was attributed to temporary nervous exhaustion or hallucination. Both the exploit and report were subsequently "unpublicized," although the fact that Byrd had made the broadcast did his reputation little good in scientific circles. Strangely enough, a number of persons who were frequent moviegoers in the twenties are sure that they remember seeing newsreels of the Byrd flight, together with views of "the land beyond the Pole," although it is possible that having read about the incident they had confused other newsreels showing the admiral's exploits with the controversial one. The incident itself has been relegated to the world of legend and is hardly ever referred to except by believers in the "hollow earth" cult, who assume that the admiral had flown into a hole in the hollow earth, rather than through a hole into another dimension as has been suggested to explain disappearances in the Bermuda Triangle.

In any event there would seem to be a similarity between the magnetic force fields, such as those allegedly created by the Philadelphia Experiment and the conditions over the Poles themselves, always assuming that Admiral Byrd's overflight of the Pole was made in circumstances when he was in complete command of his faculties.

Considering the wide choice of unusual explanations held by many serious and well-qualified investigators of the Bermuda Triangle incidents, one is somehow reminded of Haldane's epigram: "The Universe is not only queerer than we imagine, it is queerer than we *can* imagine." Among the various reasons for the chain of unexplained disappearances we have just considered, we have the selective capture of human beings by outer- or inner-space entities, a dimensional hole in the sky which planes can enter but not leave—or what has been termed "a magnetic tear in the curtain of time," and magnetic whirlpools which cause craft to disappear or perhaps move into another dimension.

These theories are neither more nor less fantastic than still another theory that predicates the existence within the Triangle of great power complexes, ancient machines or power sources from a previous civilization, lying on the ocean floor within the area of the Triangle and which even now may be occasionally triggered by overflying planes, creating magnetic vortices, and causing magnetic and electronic malfunction. The over-flying planes would therefore, in a sense, at certain times and under certain conditions, unconsciously trigger their own destruction. But while this theory is perhaps the most unbelievable (to our accepted norms) of all those suggested in this and other chapters, certain natural and unnatural features of the area in question and of the area's geological history infer a connecting thread linking through several of the above theories.

To consider this new theory we must go back in time —time in the life of the ocean and the civilization of man.

7

A Suggestion from
the Ocean's Past

IT IS GENERALLY CONSIDERED AS PROVED THAT LARGE
sections of the earth's surface were once under
water while other areas now under water were once
land. This was noted by the naturalists of ancient times,
when they found fossilized life in the desert, as well
as by modern naturalists who have found skeletons of
whales in such inland areas as Minnesota and even in
the Himalayan mountains, while ample evidence exists
that the Sahara was once an inland sea. While there is
general agreement on large-scale interchange of land
and sea throughout the world, the question of timing is
especially important for the consideration of the land
and sea level changes within the Bermuda Triangle
within comparatively recent geological times.

We know that during the Ice Age a tremendous
volume of ocean water was frozen within the several-

miles-deep glaciers that covered large parts of the Northern Hemisphere. About 12,000 years ago, when the glaciers began to melt because of climatic changes, the causes of which are not yet clear, the world's waters rose, engulfing coastal lands and islands, turning isthmuses into straits and larger islands into underwater plateaus. The old ocean water level of the earth at the time that the Third Glaciation started to melt is estimated to have been 600 feet or more below the present level. In addition, many lands once above water may lie even deeper than this because of volcanic activity taking place at the time of, or after, the flooding or, to use the biblical terminology which may have described these events—the Flood.

Almost all the world's races and tribes preserve vivid accounts of previous universal destruction by fire, flood, earthquake, explosion, or the shaking and shifting of the entire earth. In most cases, only a single survivor, along with his family and selected animals, has traditionally been spared to start a new life, as did Noah, in a new world, once the disturbances had ceased or the waters had abated. But Noah was just one survivor —the one familiar to the inheritors of Judaeo-Christian religious tradition. There were numerous survivors of the same or similar catastrophes, including Deucalion, of Greek myth, who repopulated the earth by scattering stones; Baisbasbata, the flood survivor told of in the *Mahabharata* of India; Ut-napishtim, of Babylonian legend, whose story closely resembles that of Noah; Yima, of Iran; Coxcox, of ancient Mexico, who escaped the flood in a giant cypress raft; Tezpi, of another, more developed Mexican race, who had a spacious vessel at his disposal, on which he loaded grain and animals; Bochica, of Colombian Chibcha legend, who finally got rid of the floodwaters by opening a hole in the earth (as did the Greek Deucalion); Tamandere, the guarani "Noah" of southeastern South America, who floated on a huge tree to the top of a mountain, where he survived; and many others throughout the world. In each case the animals which were saved reflect the local fauna with the general references to the animals taken on the Ark by Noah, exotically supplemented in the American legend by specific mention of such animals as llamas, jaguars, tapirs, buffalo, coyotes, and vultures saved by his ancient American counterparts.

With so specific a world legend—even the time period of the flood varies only slightly, mostly from forty to sixty days—it seems plausible to assume that a worldwide catastrophe did occur, leaving as it did so deep a trauma in the racial memory, and that it was connected with the sea, consequent changes in terrain, climate, and water levels throughout the earth.

Vestiges of this catastrophe or catastrophes are found not only in the memory of man but are witnessed by evidences of vast risings, sinkings, and bucklings of the land and the sea bottoms, such as the sandy beaches under thousands of feet of water around the Azores and coastline beaches thrust hundreds of feet upward along many coasts, especially in Greenland, Northern California, and Peru (where human artifacts are found near the bottom of ancient geological striations resulting from this upthrust). The Andes themselves, geologically fairly recent, seem to have been thrust or forced upward, perhaps carrying with them such cities as Tiahuanaco, while other coastal lands of South America dropped into the Nasca Deep in the ocean. The same catastrophe may have caused the melting of the glaciers, which thereupon flooded the plateaus of the Atlantic islands and large parts of the continental shelves, which were formerly above water. At the same time, climatic changes occurred throughout the world, evidently with startling rapidity. In Siberia, frozen bodies of mammoths are still being found, frozen so quickly that the meat proved to be edible, first by dogs, and later experimentally by Russian scientists. These mammoths, rhinoceroses, and other animals not generally associated with Siberia, were apparently entrapped in floods of freezing mud (or mud that subsequently froze) and preserved so quickly that undigested foods (of plants no longer native to Siberia) have been found in their stomachs.

Parts of Northern Siberia, Alaska, and Canada are so covered with bones of great animals that suddenly perished (again at a date estimated from 10,000 to 11,000 years ago), that some islands or high points where they went for refuge seem to be made entirely of their bones. Other survival points where completely different and inimical species fled for shelter and died in great multitudes have been found across Northern Europe, Central Asia, and China, as if the whole top of the world had experienced a rapid and unexplained climate change at the same time. However, in other hemispheres as well there are indications of the simultaneous decimation of species, from the huge elephant graveyard that exists in the Colombian Andes, and even under water, as in the case of an enormous sea elephant graveyard off the coast of Georgia. None of these animals have their natural habitats in the places where they met their deaths in such numbers in the sudden climatic change of 12,000 years ago.

Former land areas of this period now covered by water include parts of the Mediterranean, including land bridges from Africa to Gibraltar and from Sicily to Italy, a large part of the North Sea, the continental shelves off Ireland, France, the Spanish Peninsula, and Africa, the sunken plateaus around the Azores, the Canary and Madeira islands, as well as the Azores-Gibraltar ridge and the North Atlantic Ridge, and the continental shelves of North and South America, and especially the vast Bahama Banks, which, before they were submerged, covered an area of thousands of square miles.

There is abundant proof that these areas have been above the surface of the ocean within the last ten or twelve thousand years. A Russian expedition north of the Azores recently dredged rocks from 6,600 feet which gave evidence of their having been formed at atmospheric pressure about 17,000 years ago, while a nineteenth-century dredging operation, while repairing a break in the transatlantic cable in the vicinity of the Azores brought up pieces of tachylyte, a vitreous lava which forms *above* water at atmospheric pressure. The samples were estimated to be about 12,000 years old. (While this incident has often been commented on, the reason for the breaking of the cable is of special interest as an example of movements in the ocean floor—a sudden rise in the bottom of about 4,000 feet was what had caused the cable to break.)

A project now (1973–74) being carried out in the Azores by the University of Halifax for the investigation of geothermal energy has had the indirect result of ascertaining that the first 800 meters of cores drilled below sea level give indications of having been formed above sea level, with the implication that greater areas around the present Azores Islands were once above water.

Other fairly recent discoveries seem to support the time element of 12,000 years for the most recent submergence of large land areas in the Atlantic, which would also coincide with the estimated time for the Third Glaciation. In 1956 Drs. R. Malaise and P. Kolbe of the National Museum of Stockholm offered the opinion that skeletons of fresh-water diatoms, which Dr. Kolbe had brought up in a sample core from a depth of 12,000 feet near the Atlantic Ridge, had originally been deposited in a fresh-water lake, formerly on the surface of land now sunk to the bottom of the ocean. The age of these fresh-water diatoms was estimated at 10,000 to 12,000 years.

This figure is oddly coincidental with Plato's account of Atlantis in his *Timaeus* dialogue, in which he refers to a great continent having existed in the outer ocean "9,000 years ago"—or about 11,400 years before the present time.

While dates recorded from legends are suspect and even more so when they are second- or third-hand, since Plato received his information indirectly from Solon, who, on his part, originally acquired it while on a trip to Saïs in Egypt, it is nevertheless remarkable that this time calculation comes up so frequently in other fields connected with these sunken lands.

But there are still other indications that large parts of the western Atlantic were once above sea level. Beach sand, for example, is formed not at the bottom of the ocean, but by the force of waves breaking at the edge of the sea. Yet sand beaches are found on deep underwater plateaus around the Azores. Rivers form canyons only on land; yet the Hudson River canyon proceeds under water for hundreds of miles out to sea. Other river canyons extend out in like manner from where European, African, and South American rivers enter the ocean.

Mastodon and human bones have been found on the bottom of the North Sea, along with prehistoric tools, indicating a certain degree of advancement and the probability of cultural development in the Pleistocene era (prior to 11,000 B.C.). But perhaps the most striking of all indications of the drowning of cultural remains of prehistoric peoples since the melting of the last glaciers are the underwater building, walls, causeways, and roads now being found with increasing frequency under the waters of the western coasts of Europe and South Africa and the southeastern coasts of North America. The latter include underwater buildings, walls, and stone roads leading east from the coasts of Yucatán and Honduras, roads which may connect with submerged cities still farther out at sea. There is even a thirty-foot-high one-hundred-mile-long example of sea "wall" leading out into the ocean off Venezuela near the mouth of the Orinoco. This was thought at first to be a natural feature, but its straight lines and composition tend to belie this first appraisal.

There are strong indications that a continental land mass existed in the Caribbean Sea of which the islands and ridges of the Antilles may be the surviving mountain peaks. In 1969 a research expedition from Duke University studied the sea bottom of the Caribbean and conducted dredging operations at a number of places on the Aves Ridge, a ridge running along the eastern border of the oceanic Venezuelan Basin between Venezuela and the Virgin Islands. On fifty occasions granitic (acid igneous) rocks were brought to the surface. Ordinarily these rocks are found only on continents. A distinguished oceanographer, Dr. Bruce

Heezen, in commenting on this matter, has observed: "Up to now, geologists generally believed that light granitic, or acid igneous rocks are confined to the continents and that the crust of the earth beneath the sea is composed of heavier, dark-colored basaltic rock . . . Thus, the occurrence of light-colored granitic rocks may support an old theory that a continent formerly existed in the region of the eastern Caribbean and that these rocks may represent the core of a subsided, lost continent."

It is on the underwater Bahama Plateau, however, the area of the most concentrated incidents occurring within the Bermuda Triangle, that the most surprising discoveries of underwater remains have been made, and many of these at a depth of only a few fathoms. The submerged limestone formations of the Bahama Banks were largely above water about 12,000 years ago. This large land area contained bays and inland waterways which are now evident on depth maps at the deep parts of the ocean cutting in and around the Bahama Banks. This considerable land area formed, at a time previous to the rising of the sea, a large island or islands which, if we are to believe the underwater remains, supported a complex culture.

From 1968 to the present time, underwater discoveries have been made, especially near Bimini, of what seems to have been massive stonework on the present sea bottom, huge blocks of stone placed together in what may be roads, platforms, harbor works, or fallen walls. They strangely resemble the pre-Inca stonework of Peru, the pillars of Stonehenge, or the Cyclopean walls of Minoan Greece. The age of the stones is uncertain, although fossilized mangrove roots

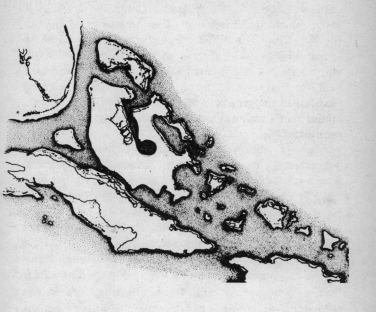

Estimated land masses formed by the present Bahama islands, Cuba, and Florida prior to the ending of the last glaciation, when waters from the melting icecap caused the oceans to rise. The present islands are shown within their former shapes. Florida, it will be noted, extended far west into the Gulf of Mexico. The dark area in the middle of the land mass formed by the present Andros, Exuma, Eleuthera, and New Providence islands is the deep ocean canyon called the Tongue of the Ocean. The sea at that time formed great island bays in the Bahamas including the present Exuma Sound and the Tongue of the Ocean.

which had grown over the stones have given carbon 14
datings of about 12,000 years.

The most celebrated of the finds has been the
Bimini "Road" or "Wall," first discovered in 1968 by
Dr. J. Manson Valentine with divers Jacques Mayol,
Harold Climo, and Robert Angove. First seen from a
boat on the surface of the water, when the sea was
especially clear and without surface movement, it was,
in the words of Dr. Valentine, "An extensive pavement
of rectangular and polygonal flat stones of varying
size and thickness, obviously shaped and accurately
aligned to form a convincingly artifactual arrangement.
These stones had evidently lain submerged over a long
span of time, for the edges of the biggest ones had become rounded off, giving the blocks the domed appearance of giant loaves of bread or pillows. Some were
absolutely rectangular, sometimes approaching perfect
squares. (One remembers that absolutely straight lines
are never present in natural formations.) The larger
pieces, at least ten to fifteen feet in length, often ran
the width of parallel-sided avenues, while the smaller
ones formed mosaic-like pavements covering broader
sections. . . . The avenues of apparently fitted stones
are straight-sided and parallel; the long one is a clear-
cut double series interrupted by two expansions containing very large, flat stones propped up at the corners
by vertical members (like the ancient dolmens of
western Europe); and the southeast end of this great
roadway terminates in a beautifully curved corner; the
three short causeways of accurately aligned large stones
are of uniform width and end in *corner* stones. . . .

"From the air, one can dimly make out, under their
blanketing of dark algae, the huge individual stones

that precisely border the margins of this geological or archaeological challenge."

The first underwater discoveries in Bimini have come under considerable attack from geologists and archaeologists, some of whom have not visited the site, but recent findings that the gigantic construction makes a turn and appears at other places on the ocean bottom, as if it once ran around Bimini and beyond, indicate the increasingly apparent size, and ramifications of this enormous structure, the purpose of which we can as yet only guess. The discoverer has expressed his personal feelings: ". . . The suggestion that the stones represent the remnants of walls, roads, or even an ancient seaport are unacceptable at the present time because it has not yet been established what, if anything besides bedrock, lies below. However, recent observations in slightly deeper water have verified multi-layered construction in at least one area. My personal feeling is that this entire complex represents the intelligent utilization, by ancient man, of materials provided by nature and appropriate for the creation of some sort of ceremonial center. In this connection it should be remembered that certain ancient sacred sites, such as the Glastonbury Circle (thirty miles in circumference), and the designs on the Nasca desert of Peru of lines and images of mile-long animals, traceable only from the air because of their gigantic proportions, have virtually no point of reference with our modern technology, as the purposes of these majestic artifacts are incomprehensible to us. . . ."

Exploratory overflights since 1968 have indicated other extraordinary and apparently man-made formations on the Bahama Banks as well as on the sea bottom near Cuba and Haiti and Santo Domingo. Some of these appear to be pyramids or tremendous dome foundations with one in the Bimini area measuring 180 by 140 feet which may be the truncated top of a pyramid, and other larger pyramids (or temple platforms) reported out at sea. Within Cuban waters a whole complex of reported underwater "ruins" is awaiting exploration, unless the Cubans themselves (Castro is an enthusiastic scuba diver) have already been there.

Two airline pilots, Bob Brush and Trig Adams, on a 1968 flight in the vicinity of Andros Island, photographed a partitioned rectangle on the Andros Shelf. Divers later found the wall to be of stone but there is no record of the original inhabitants or the later Spanish conquerors having built such constructions in that area, especially under water. What seems to be an underwater road or wall running along the top of an underwater cliff has been located and photographed near Cay Lobos. It is possible that the ancient road ran along the cliff when both were above sea level. Perhaps the underwater sighting of steps carved in the continental shelf off northern Puerto Rico, reported by the French Naval Captain Georges Houot and Lieutenant Gérard de Froberville in the bathyscaphe *Archimède* represented simply a staircase out in a rock cliff descending to the old sea level of 12,000 years ago.

Off the coast of Yucatán, Mexico, numerous road causeways have often been seen from the air. They leave the shore in straight lines toward unknown underwater locations farther out at sea in deeper waters. While connecting causeways on land are invisible because of the covering jungle, those under water are still discernible from time to time as they are uncovered by currents or storms.

What appeared to be an enormous underwater road,

or a pavement that had previously been above water, was observed from the deep-diving submarine *Aluminaut* on a 1967 mission off Florida, Georgia, and South Carolina. The road was apparently formed of, or paved with, manganese oxide and, when special wheels were installed on the *Aluminaut* it was able to proceed along the road, which in some places reached a depth of 3,000 feet, as if the *Aluminaut* were a car driving along a normal road, except that the road was, in this case, at the bottom of the sea. The size of the paved surface was too large to suggest the conclusion that it had been man-made as was also the case with a very extensive "tiled" section of the ocean bottom observed by Dr. Bruce Heezen of the Lamont Observatory, while making a deep dive in the Bahama area.

Among the apparently man-made Bermuda finds, some are clearly visible but some are apparently not only under water but under the sea bottom itself. It is a fact that stonework, or stone foundations, buried underground beneath the accumulation of ages or as the result of earthquakes or flooding will change the pattern of grass or other plant life that grows over it. This has led to some successful discoveries of the past both on land and under the sea. Vanished constructions ranging from ruined Roman camps and roads in England to ancient canal systems and city walls in what was once Babylonia and Assyria (now Iraq), and in Iran and Central Asia entire lost cities have been traced and reconstructed from the variety of pattern and shading in plant life on the ground or in marshes or under the sea. Straight lines show in the ground-cover coloration where foundations or walls are buried or where roads or canal beds have existed. The ancient Etruscan port city of Spina in Italy had so completely vanished that it was considered legendary until the traces of its walls, foundations, canals, and wharves, absolutely invisible from the ground, were clearly seen from the air.

The possibility of locating ancient sites from the air has been put to good use in the Bahamas, where the surrounding shelf is shallow enough to discern such traces of underwater constructions from the air. In many places on the Bahama Banks there are amazing assortments of great squares, rectangles, crosses, long lines parallel to each other, perhaps roads, sometimes turning at right angles, concentric circles, triangles, hexagons, and other geometrical shapes, all traced by the presence (or absence) of sea grass over the actual ruins. Underwater tests undertaken by divers indicate that the stone constructions traced by the existing bottom lines lie several feet farther down under the sand.

One may ask, with all this unusual evidence now being explored, why it was never noted before. Part of the answer is that doubtlessly it never occurred to anyone to look for a sunken civilization in the Bahama Banks, especially since so many historic sites were waiting to be found in the Mediterranean. Underwater searches in the Bahamas and off the coast of Florida have been heavily concentrated on Spanish treasure ships, certainly objects representing a more immediate financial reward than the uncovering of a forgotten and difficult to identify civilization. Even with the evidence at hand, as much effort is being spent in scientific circles to disprove the finds as by explorers and researchers to bring them to public attention. It is also to be noted that some qualified researchers are hesitant or reluctant to confront the hostile opinion of other archaeologists and oceanographers. Another element exists in that the buildings or artifacts discovered may be covered through the action of tides and storms after they have once been located, and so again lost. It is remarkable, however, that since 1968 a certain rise in the bottom of the Great Bahama Bank has taken place, uncovering traces of new formations where there were *none discernible in earlier photographs of the same area*. This was the case of a formation shaped like a large arrow, built of stone and 100 feet long, between North Cat and South Cat cays, Bimini, and another southeast of South Caicos, pointing southeast and in due alignment to another straight bottom line as yet unexplored.

Some of the already discovered sites also seem to be rising or being cleared of sediment by tidal action so that their artificial or man-made construction is more discernible. Dr. James Thorne, a distinguished oceanographer and diver, and decidedly neutral, if not skeptical, on the subject of "lost civilizations under the sea," recently examined thick columns holding up some of the stones of the Bimini "wall," a fairly convincing refutation of opinions held by numerous other oceanographers that the whole complex at Bimini and other places in the Bahamas are natural formations. Another group of divers, who had found a sunken anchor from a Spanish galleon, discovered, as they examined it and scratched at the bottom around it, that it was lying on top of a mosaic floor or terrace which may have sunk thousands of years previously.

Every time traces of a sunken civilization is found in the Atlantic (or elsewhere), a series of press and magazine articles as well as books customarily identify it with the "lost" continent of Atlantis. Atlantis, whose image has bemused mankind since antiquity, was described in considerable detail by Plato in his *Timaeus* and *Critias* dialogues as the land of the Golden Age of man, a great and wonderful world empire in the Atlantic which with ". . . violent earthquakes and floods . . . in a single day and night of rain . . . sunk beneath the sea . . . and that is the reason why the sea in those parts is impassable and impenetrable . . ."

Atlantis has, naturally enough, been identified with the Bahama underwater ruins, although Plato, as antiquity's most famous commentator on Atlantis, seems to have located it in front of the Columns of Heracles (Hercules), now known as the Straits of Gibraltar, somewhere out in the Atlantic Ocean. A close reading of Plato's account, however, will disclose a most interesting piece of information suggesting that the Atlantean Empire was no one island but a series of large islands in the Atlantic whose rule had spread to both sides of the ocean. Plato wrote:

. . . In those days [approximately 11,500 years ago] the Atlantic was navigable and there was an island situated in front of the straits which you call the Columns of Heracles: the island was larger than Libya and Asia put together, and was the way to other islands and from the islands you might pass through the whole of the opposite continent which surrounds the true ocean; for this sea which is within the straits of Heracles [the Mediterranean] is only a harbor, having a narrow entrance, but that other is the real sea and the surrounding land may be most truly called a continent.

It will be noted that Plato mentioned Libya (meaning Africa) *and* Asia but specifically and separately designates the *continent*—that is, the continent in the west which he previously mentioned as being an area of Atlantean rule.

The underwater complexes at Bimini and other points in the Bahamas have been attributed to all sorts of early ocean voyagers—Phoenicians, Carthaginians, Minoan Greeks, Mayas, Egyptians and, as a final resort as their age becomes more obvious—to Atlanteans. It is fairly sure, however, that no race within our recorded history built them and doubly sure that they were not built under water.

Plato's reference to a continent on the other side of the "true ocean" has often been cited as a proof that ancient records conserved an awareness of North America and that this memory served as an inspiration and encouragement to Columbus, who, it is reported, carried with him a map showing Atlantis and the lands beyond. Plato's account has a direct bearing on the possibility of Atlantean (used here in the sense of an Atlantic oceanic empire) presence in the extreme western part of the Atlantic Ocean. This would include the present islands of the Great Bahama Banks when large areas of the banks were well above water with the deepest present oceanic features such as the Tongue of the Ocean and the Straits of Florida forming an island bay and a sea barrier from the Florida coastline which also extended much farther out to sea. Circular declivities on the sea bottom fourteen miles off the Florida Keys and 500 feet deep from the surrounding sea bottom, which is almost 1,000 feet deep in that area, charted by the U. S. Coast and Geodetic Survey, have been assessed as fresh-water lakes covered by the sea at the time of the last rising of the ocean or sinking of the coastal lands.

A look at the present depth table of the western

Atlantic presents a clear indication that, if the sea level were lowered 600 to 800 feet, great islands would exist in the Atlantic where there are now small ones. And it is of peculiar interest to recollect that this rising of the waters took place between 11,000 and 12,000 years ago, coinciding with the account Plato reputedly received through Solon from Egyptian priests at Saïs whose written records antedated those of the Greeks by thousands of years.

Atlantis, through the course of the years, has been "located" in a number of different parts of the world; under the Atlantic Ocean, the Aegean, Caspian, and North seas, Western Africa, Spain, Tunisia, Germany, Sweden, the Sahara, Arabia, Mexico, Yucatán, Venezuela, the Azores, Canary and Madeira islands, Brazil, Ireland, Ceylon, and even under the Indian Ocean, often depending on the nationality and, one may say, the *Weltanschauung* of the writer or investigator.

The candidacy of the western part of the Bermuda Triangle as a location for Atlantis has been popularized since the 1968 discoveries by a most unusual set of circumstances, tied in with the very year of their discovery. These concern the prophecies of Edgar Cayce, the "sleeping prophet" and psychic healer who died in Virginia in 1945, but whose "readings" (a term used for interviews given while Cayce was in a trance) have continued to influence many thousands of people. While he was alive he gave through his readings advice and counsel to more than 8,000 people, first on health problems and subsequently on a variety of other matters. The documentation of his remarkable cures and telepathic powers need not be recounted here, except for what may prove to be history's most unusual archae-

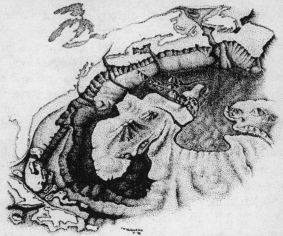

Undersea elevation of the western Atlantic Ocean bottom showing deepest areas as the darkest. Mountains in the center show Bermuda on the great pleateau called the Bermuda Rise. The deep area to the west is the Hatteras Abyssal Plain and to the south the Nares Abyssal Plain. The boundaries of the Sargasso Sea may be followed starting from the Nares Deep, up through the Hatteras Deep, turning east at the northern part of the Bermuda Rise, and south as it approaches the Mid-Atlantic Ridge and then west again back to the Nares Plain. Off the coast of the United States two great river canyons, now under water, may be seen continuing from the Hudson and Delaware rivers out under the sea through canyons made in the continental shelf. The continental shelf of the American continent and the shelves of the Antilles and the Bahama islands, the plateau around Bermuda, and the high mountains and plateaus beginning at the extreme right of the map were all presumably above water before the end of the last glaciation, and would have given the western Atlantic a totally different shape about 12,000 years ago.

ological predictions, which directly concern Atlantis and Bimini.

Between the years of 1923 to 1944 Cayce gave hundreds of trance interviews about Atlantis relating to people who, in his opinion, and that of those who have carried on his work in the Association for Research and Enlightenment, lived in Atlantis during a former life. When he was not in a trance Cayce was either unaware or uninterested in the question of Atlantis and often expressed a certain perplexity that he had mentioned it in so many readings. However, in June 1940, in connection with numerous other previous observations about Atlantis having existed in the area of Bimini (referred to by Cayce as Poseidia), he unexpectedly declared:

> Poseidia will be among the first portions of Atlantis to rise again—expected in '68—and '69—not so far away.

This curious archaeological prophecy was fulfilled almost on schedule with the numerous finds on the Bahama Banks, the uncovering by the tides of some constructions, and a rise in the bottom in certain areas. One is tempted, however, to wonder whether these discoveries were made as foretold by the prophecies or *because* of the prophecies, or because those who had read Cayce were searching for them as was the case with some of the pilots who sighted the first underwater formations or constructions.

As can be expected, the discoveries of the underwater complexes in 1968 and thereafter, as foretold twenty-eight years previously, have caused many people to examine Cayce's other references to Atlantis and the area with renewed interest. If Cayce's readings and ancient legends were based on memories of actual occurrences, one might envisage the possibility of forces developed by a former scientifically advanced civilization still being in part operative within the area where they were once concentrated and considered the possibility that the electronic, magnetic, and gravitational aberrations of the Bermuda Triangle may be a legacy, albeit a negative one, from a culture so far back in time that almost no traces remain, and our memories of it are more instinctive than concrete.

8

The Surprises of Prehistory

S EVERAL INVESTIGATORS OF THE BERMUDA TRIANGLE
mystery have suggested that alien intelligences
may be interested or even concerned in the possibility
that our development of nuclear fission for warfare may
be threatening the existence of civilization on our planet
as it may have previously destroyed other civilizations
on this and other planets.

The time span of rational man on this planet, of an
intelligence potential comparable to that of today, may
extend back 40,000 to 50,000 years in time or even
farther. Therefore, if we give a civilization such as the
present one a period of about 10,000 years to progress
to a point in science and technology where it attains
the potential of effecting its own destruction we still
have an ample time slot for the presence of one or
more world cultures antedating our own. Perhaps any
advanced technical civilization would eventually, by

chance or design, develop the power inherent in nuclear fission (it took our own civilization considerably less than 10,000 years), at which point the civilization would have to decide on a means of controlling its development or risk its own ruin. If such a world culture had existed, caused its own destruction, and disappeared, its memory would perhaps be preserved in legends, or suggested by certain anachronistic artifacts of uncertain age, or recalled by huge ruins impossible to identify or explain. And these are the very elements that tend to locate the site of such a culture in the area now covered by the waters of the Bermuda Triangle.

Edgar Cayce, in his dictated readings on Atlantis, repeatedly made what seems to be references to nuclear power sources, lasers and masers, comparable with our own and generally employed for the same uses that we enjoy (if that is the right word) today. His descriptions of their applications and his observation of the danger of their misuses would be considered today fairly standardized reporting of facts and editorial comment but—how did Cayce know all this more than thirty-five years ago?

Cayce described these power sources in some detail. They were great generators producing power to propel air and underwater craft. They were capable of producing illumination, heating, and communication. They powered forms of radio, television, and were used in long-distance photography. They also supplied the power which served for the modification and rejuvenation of living tissues, including the brain, and in this connection were also used to control and discipline entire social classes.

However, through the misuse of the natural forces they had developed, and through civil and external strife, the Atlanteans eventually unleashed uncontrollable forces of nature which caused their own destruction, a belief generally shared in common by Cayce and the legends of many older cultures of the world. In Cayce's words:

. . . Man brought in the destructive forces . . . that combined with those natural resources of the gases, of forces made in nature and natural form, the worst of the eruptions that awoke from the depth of the slowly cooling earth and that portion [of Atlantis] now near what would be termed the Sargasso Sea first went into the ocean . . .

In his relation of prehistory, Cayce seems to have specifically predicted the use of lasers and masers, whose recognized existence at that moment (in 1942) still lay some years ahead in the future. He described a gigantic crystal power source

. . . in which the light appeared as a means of communication between infinity and the finite or the means whereby there were the communications with those forces from the outside. Later this came to mean that from which the energies radiated, as of the center from which there were the radial activities guiding the various forms of transition and travel through those periods of activity of the Atlanteans.
    It was set as a crystal though in quite a different form from that [first] used there. Do not confuse these two . . . for there were many *generations* of difference. It was in those periods when there was the directing of areoplanes or means of travel though they at that time would travel in the air, or on the water, or under the water, just the same. Yet the force from which these were directed was in the central power

station—or Tuaoi stone which was . . . and the beam
on which it acted . . .

In another reading, he referred to a location in
"Poseidia," in other words, the Bahamas area, then
above water, as the site of:

> . . . the storage of the *motivative* forces of nature
> from the great crystals that so condensed the lights,
> the forms, the activities, as to guide not only the ships
> on the sea but in the air and of many of those now
> known conveniences for man as in the transmission
> of the body, and in the transmission of the voice, as
> in the recording of those activities in what is soon to
> become a practical thing in so creating the vibra-
> tions as to make for television—as it is termed in
> the present. [The "present," in this case, refers to
> 1935!]

A 1932 "reading" contains an interesting reference
to transportation of heavy weights and materials:

> . . . Through the use of . . . those recently redis-
> covered gasses and those of the electrical and aeriatic
> formations in the breaking up of the atomic forces to
> produce impelling force to those means and modes
> of transportation or of travel, or of lifting large
> weights, or of changing the forces of nature itself.

The fact that the supposedly primitive peoples of
prehistory have left enormous stones still in place after
thousands of years, upon many of which subsequent
races have built new constructions, has long been an
archaeological mystery, since the stones set by unknown
preceding races are so much larger and more difficult to
transport than those put in place by subsequent cultures

that their presence and mode of transportation are un-explainable. Examples include the 200-ton porphyry blocks of Ollantaytambo and Ollantayparubo, Peru, transported great distances over mountains and ravines and then placed on the tops of other cliffs 1,500 feet high. The enormous blocks of Sacsahuaman, Peru, so large and so intricately faced flush one to the other that the Incas attributed their construction to the gods; the 100-ton *foundation* blocks of Tiahuanaco, Bolivia, on which enormous buildings were somehow constructed, although the altitude is two and a half miles above sea level. Other examples include the great stones of the calendar or observatory at Stonehenge, England, the massive blocks of the Bimini undersea wall, foundation, or sea bastion, or the standing stones of prehistoric Brittany, one of which weighed over 340 tons and stood sixty-five feet high, and the great stones of the foundation of the Temple of Jupiter at Baalbek, Syria, placed there long before the classical temple was built, one of which weighs 2,000 tons. As almost all of these constructions are extremely difficult to explain in terms of our assessment of the engineering skills of the cultures that we *think* erected them, it has been suggested that a superior civilization was responsible for their construction. This is supported by the fact that many of these inexplicable ruins closely resemble each other.

Cayce specifically singled out Bimini as one of the several points where information concerning the alleged power sources of Atlantis was to be found: ". . . In the sunken position of Atlantis or Poseidia, where a portion of the temples may be discovered under the slime of ages of seawater—near what is known as Bimini off the coast of Florida."

A detailed description of one of these power sources

(or nuclear plants?) was transcribed in 1935. Cayce's son, Edgar Evans Cayce, a practicing engineer and also an author (*Edgar Cayce on Atlantis,* Warner Library, 1968), has observed, in commenting on the paradox of Cayce's accounts of prehistory having predated by some decades our own scientific developments: "A layman of today could scarcely describe our latest scientific developments more clearly." Cayce's account (recorded in 1933) deals with a building where the "firestone" or crystal complex was kept and from which its power was diffused:

In the center of a building which today would be said to be lined with nonconductive stone—something akin to asbestos, with . . . other nonconductors such as are now being manufactured in England under a name which is well known to many of those who deal in such things.

The building above the stone was oval; or a dome wherein there could be . . . a portion for rolling back, so that the activity of the stars—the concentration of energies that emanate from bodies that are on fire themselves, along with elements that are found and not found in the earth's atmosphere.

The concentration through the prisms or glass (as would be called in the present) was in such manner that it acted upon the instruments which were connected with the various modes of travel through induction methods which made much the (same) character of control as would in the present day be termed remote control through radio vibrations or directions; through the kind of force impelled from the stone acted upon the motivating forces in the crafts themselves.

The building was constructed so that when the dome was rolled back there might be little or no hindrance in the direct application of power to various crafts that were to be impelled through space—whether within the radius of vision or whether directed underwater or under other elements, or through other elements.

The preparation of this stone was solely in the hands of the initiates at the time; and the entity was among those who directed the influences of the radiation which arose, in the form of rays that were invisible to the eye but acted upon the stones themselves as set in the motivating forces—whether the aircraft were lifted by the gases of the period; or whether for guiding the more-of-pleasure vehicles that may pass along closer to the earth, or crafts on the water or under the water.

These, then, were impelled by the concentration of rays from the stones which were centered in the middle of the power station or powerhouse (as would be the term in the present).

Cayce constantly returns to the misuse of the tremendous forces developed by this super-civilization—". . . the raising of the powers from the sun itself to the ray that makes for the disintegration of the atom . . . brought about the destruction of that portion of the land."

If, and always if, such a cataclysm or series of cataclysms occurred, the great power source would have been precipitated into the sea, along with the populous cities, walls, canals, and other constructions of Atlantis. It is interesting to consider that the very sites indicated by this theory are those where many of the electromagnetic aberrations in the Bermuda Triangle have taken place, such as the Tongue of the Ocean, Bimini, and other locations.

While such power complexes could hardly be expected to function after thousands of years, it is never-theless interesting in this connection to comment on the behavior of the mysterious "white waters" noted by observers from Columbus to the astronauts. The flumes of white water appear to originate at the same point or points of emanation, line up the same way, and then drift off for a mile or more. The lines are squiggly at the beginning and then become less definite, almost as if they indicated gases escaping under pressure.

Compass deviations and electric malfunction might be caused by an enormous concentration of metal under the water. This has been observed in various parts of the world where known deposits of iron cause com-passes to vary. Subsurface or substratum masses can possibly affect even the surface of the sea. In a 1970 NASA report of a "cavity" on the surface of the ocean above the Puerto Rico Trench, the surface depression was attributed by scientists to "an unusual distribution of mass beneath the ocean floor," causing deflection of the pull of gravity. In the case of the Bermuda Triangle it has been suggested that ruined sources of power have still conserved some of their strength and, triggered at certain times, might not only be responsible for mag-netic and electronic deviation but also contribute electri-cal impulses for magnetic storms.

This theory, one of the most unusual of those pro-posed to explain the Bermuda Triangle incidents, is predicated on Cayce's readings and a belief in them. However, one may justifiably ask, is there any reason for the scientifically curious to credit *any* of Cayce's recorded statements other than to admire them as the product of a vivid imagination? While it is true that some of the power sources he described thirty-five years ago were not yet discovered or even imagined in the "real world" (and some have not yet been developed), it must be remembered that Cayce was not a physicist. Nor was he a historian. He was simply a clairvoyant healer with an excellent record. However, predictions that have nothing to do with healing which he made in the course of his readings have somehow proved uncomfortably exact, such as the atom bomb, the assassination of U. S. Presidents, racial turmoil in the United States, and even mud slides in California.

In addition, Cayce's readings are purportedly based on visions or memories from his subjects' lives during their past incarnations, a feature which frequently has ruled out credibility on the part of persons who, from religion, scientific conviction, or their own logic, do not accept the theory of reincarnation. One wonders if there might be an alternate explanation which might account for such detailed and scientifically valid descriptions of past civilizations and their potentially dangerous developments.

In the religious and philosophical records of ancient India, which often contain strangely modern concepts of matter and the universe, we find references to what is called "cosmic consciousness," meaning the persistent presence of memories of everything that has happened before. Today the existence of telepathy, the influence and hidden persistence of memory, and the power of psychic emanations, far from being downgraded by modern scientific investigation, are being seriously studied, not only on earth but also in space both as phenomena and also as means of communication. Experiments are being conducted by the leading space powers, the United States and the U.S.S.R., that suggest that science fiction may be undergoing a metamorphosis into a future science fact. It is possible to expect surprisingly new developments in this area in which up to now certain gifted individuals have had, almost without being conscious of it, the ability to pick up the thoughts of others in the present and perhaps their hidden memories of the past. The past, in this case, could refer to memories inherited in chromosomes from our ancestors. For, just as we inherit physical attributes and tendencies from our parents and grandparents, we also inherit them, to a lesser degree perhaps, from our distant ancestors, and these memory chromosomes may be a part of this legacy. There is ample room within the human brain (of which only an estimated 10 per cent is used) for the storage of an inherited memory bank.

This would tend to explain the presence of a person's incomplete memories, the poignant sense of having visited a place before, where one knows one has not been in this lifetime, the frustrating certainty of having lived an extended period of time within a single dream, the recall by persons, sometimes but not always under hypnosis, of details of past lives (which have often been verified as historically accurate when previously unknown information about the time period in question was discovered), the cases of sudden fluency in and subsequent forgetfulness by children of languages spoken by their ancestors but whose use they could not possibly have acquired. While consideration of these known factors are often attributed to the reincarnation of souls, a belief shared by Buddhism, Hinduism, and the religion which perhaps had the longest life in religious history, that of ancient Egypt, the suggestion of inherited memory offers a possible alternative, although it really approximates the same thing, somewhat modified if we consider that rather than the individual's soul being that of some chance person in time it is our own ancestors who are reincarnated in us, endowing us with their accumulated memories, along with their other attributes, just as "generations" of computers can be programmed to install their total memory banks into succeeding new machines.

However, whether Edgar Cayce effectively communicated with the reincarnated souls or the reincarnated memories of the people he served, the effect was much the same and the interest in Atlantis generated by his readings has given the whole subject a new impetus, constantly increasing as unexpected discoveries within the last decade or so have seemed to offer a remarkable substantiation of the Atlantean readings.

Those who hold to the theory that there existed a highly developed world civilization before the first culture stirrings in Egypt and Sumeria have long been considered cultists, sensationalists, visionaries, or simply fools. This reaction from what we might call "the establishment" of archaeological or prehistoric studies is understandable when we consider that the existence of a great civilization before the third millennium B.C. would considerably upset the neat tables and progressive steps of history from its early beginnings in Egypt and Mesopotamia, through the cultures of Greece and Rome eventually culminating in our own "super-civilization" of today. Passing acknowledgment is often accorded to other little-known ancient cultures as, for example, the prehistoric civilization of the Americas, India, Central Asia, and certain other areas which did not, in any case, affect our own "direct line" of civilization.

Although there exists an abundance of legends and records in all ancient cultures concerning the sudden annihilation of a great civilization before the Flood, which had progressed so far as to challenge heaven, the gods, or God, these legends, however strangely similar among themselves, may simply represent an object lesson or interesting story spread throughout the world in ancient marketplaces and along caravan trails or shipping routes for thousands of years and subsequently preserved within the religious records of almost all the earth's peoples. Legends of a universal flood, a tower that men tried to build to heaven, and whose workers were confounded by a divinely inspired confusion of languages, as well as other familiar stories, were found by the invading Spaniards already to exist in the Indian civilization of the Americas at the time of the first Spanish conquest. Throughout the world legends preserved by indigenous populations still dwelling within the shadow of enormous ruins, whose construction could not have been engineered except by stone setting and transportation techniques of an extremely advanced technology, refer always to a godlike race which moved the huge stones many thousands of years before their own history began. There are even traces of what might have been an ancient trade language, possibly an ancestor of ancient Greek with Aramaic overtones, found in language areas so far removed from the Middle East that they seem to have been washed up on the most distant shores by the seas and oceans. These include words of an archaic Greek in Hawaiian and other Polynesian languages, in the Maya language of Yucatán, in Nahuatl, the language of the Aztecs, and the lost Guanche language of the Canary Islands, spoken by a mysterious white race. (The Guanches, discovered and soon exterminated by Spanish expeditions in the fifteenth century, had preserved memories of a larger homeland with a superior culture that had sunk beneath the ocean.) The ancient American languages also contained words of clearly Aramaic and Phoenician origin as well as some analogous to those contained in the Sinitic and Polynesian languages from the other side of the Pacific, all indicative of long voyages and cultural contacts of extreme antiquity. Inscriptions in Phoenician, Aramaic, Minoan, Greek, and unidentified languages are being found with increasing frequency in North and South American jungle or "second growth" areas. But legends, religious myths, and linguistic curiosities are not enough in themselves to inspire belief in the allegations made in the Cayce records as well as in tribal traditions, legends, and even the written records of antiquity concerning highly developed scientific knowledge, and the existence, in archaic times, of various modern conveniences concerning travel, communication, and destruction on a cosmic scale.

It is precisely in these areas, however, that unusual discoveries and re-evaluation of previously discovered material have been made in the past few years. They concern amazing indications of the advanced knowledge and sophisticated inventions belonging to an era long before what history tells us were the beginning of the first cultures of the Middle East. It is interesting to remember in this regard that the legends of Egypt and Sumeria both referred to a prior greater culture from which they drew their own inspiration and impetus. In some cultures, as in the cases of ancient Egypt, Bolivia, Peru, Central America, Mexico, and India, to mention but a few, civilization remained static or retrogressed instead of sustaining the original impetus.

A serious suggestion that extremely ancient cultures on this earth were familiar with "heavier-than-air machines" is one which normally would be greeted with

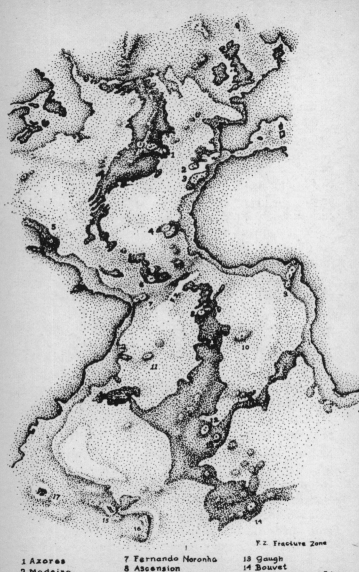

1 Azores	7 Fernando Noronha	13 Gough
2 Madeira	8 Ascension	14 Bouvet
3 Canaries	9 Guinea Ids.	15 South Georgia Ids.
4 Cape Verdes	10 St. Helena	16 S. Sandwich Ids.
5 Lesser Antilles	11 Trinidade	17 Falklands
6 St. Peter a. Paul	12 Tristan da Cunha	

F.Z. Fracture Zone

derision. Nevertheless, an increasing number of artifacts and written references have either been discovered or re-examined in recent years which indicated an awareness or even familiarity with aircraft and air travel at an era considerably before what we considered the dawn of history. Nor are these reports or models to be compared with the picturesque references of ancient mythology, such as Icarus with his feathered wings held together with wax, or the sun chariot of Apollo, drawn by four fiery steeds. On the contrary, they are concrete references which demonstrate a knowledge of aerodynamics and an awareness of the factors of takeoff, propulsion, braking, and landing.

For example, in the antique gold collection of the Republic of Colombia, there exists a golden model of what had long been considered a bird, moth, or flying fish, found in a tomb with other buried objects which were estimated as being at least 1,800 years old. This artifact was subsequently examined under magnification by Ivan Sanderson, who suspected that it was not a model of a living organism, but a model of a mechanical object, strongly resembling a plane with delta wings,

The Atlantic Ridge, showing connections with South America and Africa, interrupted only by the equatorial "fracture zone" (f.z.). Oceanic islands associated with the ridge are shown numbered on the legend on the lower right. Some of these islands may have formed considerable land areas when the ocean level was lower, about 12,000 years before the present era, forming at that time the extensive Atlantic islands described by Plato, including "Atlantis." Oceanic deeps are shown as white areas on either side of the range. (The 2,000-fathom contour line issued here for the continental shelves and intercontinental ridges.)

engine housing, a cockpit, and windshield, all in what would be the correct location in a modern plane, and having also a flanged tail and ailerons, or elevators. This object was checked with several pilots and engineers, including J. A. Ullrich, an experienced pilot with combat service in two wars and a professor of aerodynamics. When he was asked what it was, Ullrich, unaware of its provenance, or that it had previously been considered a model of a bird, insect, or fish, stated that it seemed at first to be a model of an F-102 fighter plane and that the fact that the wings curled down at their ends, as well as the shape of the plane, indicated that it was a jet. He noted that some features, such as the lack of rear elevators, not part of the F-102, were similar to those of the new Sabre aircraft recently developed in Sweden. Part of his opinion is especially interesting in view of Cayce's mention of vehicles which could fly through the air and *under the sea,* as well as reports from the Bermuda Triangle area concerning UFOs sometimes entering and leaving the water at great speeds. In Ullrich's words:

> The configuration is only valid for certain types of flight—high nose altitude. The type of wing is suitable for atmosphere up to fifty to sixty thousand feet. . . . The sweep is to prevent vibrations when passing the sound barrier. . . . The wing structure indicates supersonic abilities. . . . When you fly at super speed you build up a cushion. . . . It would also be able to fly underwater and not tear off the wings. In order to move a craft at high speed through such a medium it would be [constructed] like this.

But this "plane," if such it is, is not a unique archaeological freak. Other examples, some with two sets of wings, have since been found in different pre-Columbian tombs. One can only guess what other curious models of mechanical developments from prehistoric eras, perhaps not even recognized as such by their later users, were lost when the Spanish invaders melted down all the gold artifacts they could locate to make them into bars for easier distribution among the conquerors.

Pictorial representations of what appear to be aircraft or rockets have increasingly been identified or recognized in the art of the ancient cultures of the Americas. As most of the written or pictorial records of the civilized nations were destroyed by the Spaniards, these references have been preserved in other ways—sometimes etched on rock, painted on a vase, carved in stone, or woven in cloth used for mummy wrappings. There is an especially striking example in a half-reclining Maya figure carved in stone on the lid of a sarcophagus found deep within a pyramid in Palenque, Mexico. It is not known what the detailed carving represents; one Maya authority says the bottom is an earth monster on which a figure is resting while the whole seems to be topped by a tree. The Russian scientific writer Alexander Kazantsev has suggested a more revolutionary explanation. He believes that the reclining figure is enclosed within a stylized space vehicle, comparable in construction and design to the rockets of today. Even the position of the figure of the man (or pilot) is indicative of the position in which our astronauts are placed within the rocket and all features from the antenna through the flight direction system, turbo compressor, control panel, fuel tanks, combustion chamber, turbine, and exhaust are recognizable although modified for aesthetic effect. One has the feeling that these representations of aircraft and rockets are reminders or memories of an era of higher civilization, when such craft would be drawn exactly rather than stylistically.

In August of 1973, the astronauts of Skylab 2, while in their space orbit, received a most unusual assignment. They were to photograph, if possible, the Nasca Lines, a series of mysterious artificial lines in the Nasca Valley of Peru, to see whether they were visible from space. These enormous ground markings form a series of straight lines and geometric figures, huge drawings of animals visible only from the air, as well as what clearly seem to be several landing strips for aircraft. They were incised into the ground or chipped into the rocky floor of the valley at an unknown time in the past. There were no local legends about them and, since they were not noticeable at ground level, they were discovered only from the air during a search for water resources in the Andes. The lines and gigantic drawings fill a large part of the Nasca Valley, sixty miles long and ten miles deep. Sometimes they disappear in front of small mountains and come out absolutely straight on the other side. Sometimes designs, as in the case of the presumed landing fields, are extremely wide and sometimes they form huge, artistically sophisticated pictures of animals, fish, and birds, and even an enormous spider. While theories of their origin are many, the only self-evident one is that they were made by people who possessed highly developed instruments for reckoning and that they were made to be seen from the sky, as this is the only way that one can follow their form.

On the Bay of Pisco on the Peruvian coast there is a high rock wall on which is incised an enormous trident or candelabrum, according to the interpretation of the viewer, which, unlike the Nasca Lines (it is over

800 feet long), was easily seen from the sea by the invading Spaniards, who interpreted it as a sign of the Trinity to encourage them to the conquest and conversion of the heathens. Whatever its purpose was, it is more noticeable from the air than from the sea and the central tine of the trident points directly to the Nasca Valley, as if it were a direction indicator to the so-called "landing fields," perhaps themselves bases for the planes whose golden models are so perplexing.

Other geometric lines and enormous figures apparently designed to be seen from the air exist in other parts of the Americas in varied locations, such as huge humanoid figures in the Tarapacá Desert in Chile, the Navajo Maze in California, the Elephant and Serpent mounds of Wisconsin, as well as others in different parts of the world, often with no previous archaeological history.

The great storehouse of archaeology, pharaonic Egypt, has only recently revealed some surprising indications of the principles of heavier-than-air flight in antiquity. Unlike the golden airplanes of Colombia, these are made of wood, found in tombs where they were preserved from decay for thousands of years by the dry climate of Egypt. What appear to be models of glider planes have been found in museum collections where they had previously been considered to be models of birds, discovered in ancient tombs. A wooden model now in the Egyptian Museum of Antiquities, identified and studied by Dr. Khalil Messiha in 1969, far from being a bird, possesses the same characteristics as monoplane aircraft models of today. The rudder or tail is upright and the body has an aerofoil section. In commenting on the dihedral angles noticeable on either side, Dr. Messiha's brother, G. Messiha, a flight engineer, has observed:

> The negative dihedral angle fulfills the same requirements as the positive; a section shows that the surface of the wing is part of an ellipse which provides stability in flight; and the aerofoil shapes of the body lessens the drag, a fact which was discovered after years of experimental work in aeronautics.

The airplane, after thousands of years, is still capable of flight and, when thrown from the hand like a model glider, performs admirably, demonstrating the knowledge of aerodynamics on the part of its ancient makers. Since Dr. Messiha first realized that the wingspreads of some of the bird models were almost identical to the wingspread of the new Caravelle aircraft, other potential planes or gliders were identified and, in 1972, an exhibition of fourteen such models was opened at the Cairo Museum of Antiquities as a proof of the knowledge of flight in ancient Egypt. We do not know whether these artifacts were invented, or inherited from an older culture. However, as most Egyptian tomb models are linked to larger originals, it is possible that under the desert sands an original glider or aircraft may await the excavator.

The most complete of the ancient written records concerning aircraft are perhaps those of the *Mahabharata,* the Hindu epic that, although considered to have been written down in its present form in 1500 B.C., was apparently copied and recopied from remote antiquity. The epic deals with the actions of the gods and of the ancient peoples in India but contains such a wealth of detail of a scientific nature that, when it

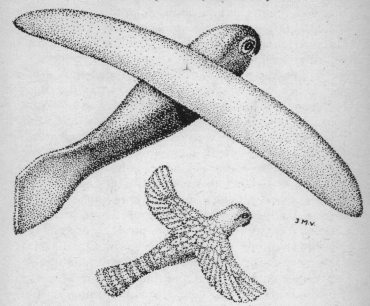

*Ancient Egyptian glider plane found in a tomb, origi-
nally thought to be a model of a bird, as compared with
an ancient model of a hawk. The plane (left) suggests
a knowledge on the part of the makers of the principles
of aerodynamics, demonstrating camber, the angle of
wing sweep back from the fuselage, and the dihedral
angle, the angle of lift or depression in regard to the
fuselage. The tail of the plane is vertical—a feature
never seen in birds. The wings of the glider are formed
to create a vacuum for lift above the wing. Although
they have principles of flight in common, birds, with
movable feathered wings and tails, are built differently
from planes, and the construction of the glider is ample
proof that it is not a model of a bird, but a model of a
heavier-than-air machine. In addition it flies a considerable distance when thrown from one's hand.*

was first translated in the middle of the nineteenth century, references to aircraft and rocket propulsion made no sense to the translators since the mechanisms described thousands of years in the past were not to make their appearance in modern times until more than half a century later. Many of the verses in the *Mahabharata* devoted to flying machines called *vimanas* contained, to the mystification of the translators, detailed information on the principles of their construction. In another ancient Indian text, the *Samarangana Sutradhara,* the advantages and disadvantages of different types of aircraft are discussed at length as to their relative capabilities of ascent, cruising speed, and descent, and even a description of the fuel power source—mercury—and recommendations regarding types of wood and light, heat-absorbing metals suitable for aircraft construction. In addition there are informative details on how to take pictures of enemy planes, methods of determining their approach patterns, means of rendering their pilots unconscious, and finally, how to destroy enemy *vimanas.*

In another ancient classic of India, the *Ramayana,* there exist curious descriptions of travel by aircraft, thousands of years ago. Details of the view over Ceylon and parts of the Indian coast are written so naturally and are so similar to what one now sees—the breakers on the shore, the curve of the land, the rising of the hills, the aspect of towns and forests—that one is almost convinced that *some* air travelers of ancient times actually saw the earth from the sky rather than imagined it. In a contemporary abstract of the *Ramayana,* the *Mahavira Charita,* the god-hero Rama, on his return from Lanka, where he has just rescued his wife, Sita, is presented with a special *vimana,* described as: "unimpeded in its motion, of coveted speed, under complete control, whose action is ever obedient to the will . . . (of him who flies it) . . . furnished with window apartments and excellent seats . . .", an instance where an ancient classic reads like a modern advertisement for Air India. In this same text we find an exchange of dialogue which is especially startling when we remember that it preceded the actuality of space travel, as well as a realization of how things looked in space, by several thousand years:

Rama: The motion of this most excellent of chariots seems changed.

Vishishara: . . . This chariot is now abandoning its proximity to the middle world.

Sita: How is it that even in daytime there appears . . . this circle of stars?

Rama: Queen! It is indeed a circle of stars, but owing to the great distance we cannot perceive in the daytime as our own eyes are dimmed by the rays of the sun. Now that is removed by the ascent of this chariot . . . (and thus we can see the stars).

Whether these accounts are memories of a very ancient technically advanced civilization or whether they are simply fantasies comparable to some of the imaginings of present-day science fiction writers, some of these accounts from the distant past sound strangely contemporaneous except for the material used as the source of power for the aircraft (which may, of course, be mistranslated from the original):

. . . Inside it one must place the mercury engine with its iron heating apparatus beneath. By means of the power latent in the mercury which sets the driving whirlwind in motion, a man sitting inside may travel a far distance in the sky . . . four mercury containers must be built into the interior structure. When these have been heated by controlled fire . . . the *vimana* develops thunder power through the mercury . . . If this iron engine with properly welded joints be filled with mercury and the fire be conducted to the upper part, it develops power with the roar of a lion . . . and at once it becomes like a pearl in the sky . . .

But models and pictures of aircraft and accounts of rockets and space flights are only an indication, not a proof, of high scientific advancement. However, certain techniques and artifacts, some recognized many years after their discovery for what they really were, furnish a more tangible proof of a previously unsuspected technological capability of the distant past.

A good example is that of the Antikythera "star computer," a small bronze object consisting of plates and wheels or dials fused together by the sea, picked up, along with other objects, mostly statues, from an ancient wreck on the floor of the Aegean Sea over seventy years ago. Subjected to detailed examination and acid baths almost sixty years later and through the studies of several archaeologists including Derek de Solla Price and George Stamires, it turned out to be a geared star finder and computer of planetary orbits, a mechanism for checking positions at night, indicating unsuspected navigational and astronomical knowledge in ancient times. In the words of Dr. Price: ". . . Nothing like this instrument is preserved elsewhere . . . Finding a thing like this is like finding a jet plane in the tomb of King Tut . . ."—an eventuality perhaps not completely outside the bounds of possibility in the light of recent findings.

Other concrete proofs of technical advancement may still lie within museums, classified as religious objects, children's toys, or simply labeled "unclassified." Wilhelm König, a German archæologist, digging at a 2,000-year-old site near Baghdad in Iraq, shortly before World War II, unearthed some curious artifacts consisting of cylinders lined with asphalt, contained within jars and provided with an iron plug—in other words, dry-cell batteries without the electrolyte, which had, whatever it was, evaporated. Samples of these batteries later functioned perfectly when a new electrolyte—copper sulphate—was added. After his initial find König identified parts of other batteries already on display in museums and labeled as of "unknown use." Since these batteries were excavated and identified many other ancient examples have been found in Iraq and other parts of the Middle East. They were apparently used for electroplating metals, but one wonders if this extremely ancient knowledge of electricity, perhaps inherited from an early culture but forgotten until it was rediscovered in the eighteenth century, was used in ancient times for purposes other than electroplating. The Greek and Roman world used torches and oil lamps for illumination and wherever passageways are still standing between ancient buildings traces of smoke can be found on the ceilings. But, in the case of the more remote Egyptian civilization, subterranean tunnels, beautifully carved and painted, show no traces of torches or oil lamps on the ceilings, nor do the walls and ceilings of certain caves in western Europe where the remarkably sophisticated Magdalenian and Aurignacian cave painters executed their masterpieces 12,000 to 30,000 years ago.

An ancient Egyptian wall carving at the Temple of Hathor at Dendera, Egypt, long considered to be rather an archaeological puzzle, depicts a scene were attendants seem to be carrying giant light bulbs, with interior filaments in the shape of thin snakes, connected to a box or switch with braided cables, and which strongly suggest powerful electric lamps supported by high-tension insulators. Regarding the cables, Dr. John Harris of Oxford has observed:

. . . The cables are virtually an exact copy of engineering illustrations as currently used. The cable is shown as very heavy and striated, indicating a bundle of many (multipurpose) conductors rather than a single high voltage cable . . .

There exist other illustrations in papyrus and in carvings, preserved for thousands of years by the dry climate of Egypt, which, when looked at with a fresh and unbiased approach, seem quite evidently to depict ancient use of modern devices. One remembers that in the Egyptian records there is reference to the reign of the gods before the first dynasty, a time of superior civilization and miraculous powers, shared in memory and records by the most ancient world cultures.

It is surprising to realize that ancient cultures, considerably antedating Greece and Rome, possessed knowledge of astronomy, advanced mathematics, the calculation of time, and measures of the earth and solar system thousands of years before these same facts were rediscovered or re-established in modern times. To have come by this information the ancient culture or cultures

Wall carving from the Temple of Hathor at Dendera, Egypt, thousands of years old, showing what were formerly described as "ritual objects" but to a modern eye strongly resemble powerful light bulbs with braided cables attached to what may be a switch or generator. Evidence of knowledge of electricity has been found in different areas of Egypt and the ancient Middle East, together with indications of its use in electroplating and possibly also for illumination.

would have to have had telescopes or other instruments sufficiently precise as to make the exact calculations.

Extraordinary discoveries have been made in the study of certain medieval maps, notably by Professor

Charles Hapgood (*Maps of the Ancient Sea Kings*), who has spent many years re-examining these maps in the light of their containing information about the earth presumably unknown at the time the maps were made. Some of these maps have been copied and recopied through the centuries from vanished originals formerly kept in the great library of ancient Alexandria, and demonstrate startlingly accurate knowledge of lands as yet undiscovered (according to history as we have learned it) when the original and even the copies were made, such as the existence of North and South America and Antarctica thousands of years before Columbus.

The Piri Reis map, a section of a larger world map of ancient times, found in 1929 amid the clutter of the former harem of the ousted Sultan of Turkey, clearly shows the true coast of Antarctica as it *would be* without the covering ice, as well as the topography of the interior, also without the covering ice. An examination of Antarctic land cores, taken in the vicinity of the Ross Sea, indicate that Antarctica has been covered by ice for six thousand years as a minimum. This would mean that the original map was made considerably before recorded history, during the time era attributed to Atlantis and its reputed world culture.

Another map, the King Jaime World Chart of 1502, also a copy of much earlier maps, shows the Sahara Desert to be a fertile land with large lakes, rivers, and cities which, at a remote period, it once was. The Buache World Map of 1737 shows Antarctica, as copied from an ancient Greek map (and the very existence of Antarctica was only suspected by the modern world until it was officially discovered in 1820), as two large islands, separated by an inland sea. If the ice could be removed from Antarctica this is precisely how the land would look, although this was not known until expeditions made this discovery in the Geophysical Year of 1958. Other maps show some of the glaciers of the last Ice Age still existing in parts of Europe, Britain, and Ireland, and, in another, the Bering Strait is shown not as a strait but as a land isthmus, as once it was.

The salient features of these recopied maps of antiquity are the facts that their exact co-ordinates and knowledge of longitude (not developed in the modern world until the end of the eighteenth century) indicate a knowledge of spherical trigonometry and the use of geodetic instruments of excellent precision, and the possibility that they were originally plotted during a period approximately 8,000 to 10,000 years ago, many centuries before our own recorded history.

Curious bits of correct astronomical information exist in the records of ancient races although, as far as we know, they had no telescopes, giant or otherwise, to obtain such data. These include the awareness of the two moons of Mars (and their distance from the planet), the seven satellites of Saturn, the four moons of Jupiter, and the phases of Venus (called the "Horns" in Babylonian records). Even aspects of the far stars were discovered: the Scorpion constellation is so-called because it has a "tail," a comet within the constellation, but this can only be seen with a powerful telescope. On the other side of the ocean the Maya of Central America, perhaps with a shared knowledge of a previous culture, called this constellation the "Scorpion" as well. (The Maya, of all ancient peoples, computed the solar year to the closest figure reached by any calendar, including our own, as 365.2420 days, with the exact figure being 365.2422 days.)

As scientific knowledge apparently receded from its ancient apogee, much of this astronomical information became transformed into legends, as, for example, that of the god (planet) Uranus who ate (eclipsed) his own children (moons) and then disgorged (end of eclipse) them. Although such a phenomenon could no longer be seen because of the disappearance of viewing devices, the astronomical information was preserved through semi-religious myths.

Perhaps the most unusual of all the indications of a previously advanced science still extant and available for our examination is the Great Pyramid of Egypt. For thousands of years it has been reputed to be a tomb, although a tradition preserved by the Copts, an Egyptian minority directly descended from the ancient Egyptians, indicated that it was a compilation of the knowledge of the "Reign of the Gods"; and that it would prove to be a book in stone, compiled by Surid, one of the kings *before the flood,* and would be deciphered in the future by those sufficiently advanced to read it.

This hidden information aspect of the Great Pyramid was noted during the Napoleonic invasion of Egypt when French engineers, using the Great Pyramid as a triangulation point, found that the sides were exactly aligned to the cardinal points with the longitudinal meridian passing through the apex of the pyramid, and diagonal lines through the apex of the pyramid prolonged northward would exactly bisect the Nile Delta. A line extended due north through the meeting point of the base diagonals would miss the North Pole by only four miles, always considering that the North Pole could have changed its position in the centuries since the Great Pyramid was built.

Today's system of metric measurement is based on the meter, one ten-millionth of the meridian, a measurement developed by the French shortly before their invasion of Egypt. The pyramidal cubit of fifty inches employed by the ancient Egyptians and which predated the French meter by thousands of years is almost equal to the meter in length but is actually more exact in that it is based on the length of the polar axis instead of the length of any meridian, which can change somewhat according to the contours of the earth.

Certain measurements taken of the Great Pyramid in terms of the Egyptian cubit indicate an astonishing knowledge of the earth and the earth's place in the solar system—a knowledge forgotten and not rediscovered until the modern era. The information is expressed in mathematics: the perimeter of the pyramid is equivalent to the count of days in the year, 365.24; doubling the perimeter gives the equivalent of one minute of one degree at the Equator; the distance from the base to the apex on the slant of the side is one six-hundredth of a degree of latitude; the height multiplied by 10^9 gives the approximate distance from the earth to the sun; the perimeter divided by twice the height of the pyramid gives the value of π, 3.1416 (considerably more exact than the figure arrived at by ancient Greek mathematicians—3.1428); the weight of the pyramid multiplied by 10^{15} gives the approximate weight of the earth. The earth's polar axis changes in space from day to day (bringing a new constellation of the zodiac behind the sun every 2,200 years), and reaches its original position once in 25,827 years, a figure which appears in the pyramidal calculations

(25,826.6) when the cross diagonals of the base are added together. The measurements of the King's Chamber within the Great Pyramid give the exact dimensions of the two basic Pythagorean triangles: 2.5.3 and 3.4.5, although it was built several thousand years before Pythagoras. And these are only a few of the pyramid's coincidental measurements.

One wonders why such a huge and complicated structure should be raised to impart such information unless, following a series of global catastrophes, survivors still possessed of technological facilities wished to pass on knowledge to the future in a way that could not be destroyed, even if all records and all languages then existing were lost. In this connection one is reminded of the suggestion that when explorers from space reach Earth or space probes from Earth reach other civilized planets, mathematics and mathematical equations would be an effective means of establishing primary communication, as the scientific and technological background for such a trip would be necessarily based on mathematics. The Pyramid's message, not from the future but from our own past, may in future reveal considerably more elements of information as we become more expert in recognizing them.

It has sometimes been suggested by researchers of the Great Pyramid as well as by Coptic tradition that the Great Pyramid is a record of a body of knowledge which was later dispersed or lost, except that part of it that was preserved in legends. Such vestiges of a prior worldwide civilization or civilizations that we think we can recognize seem to indicate that, while some of their developments were similar to ours, they may have developed in other fields with which we are as yet largely unfamiliar. Tremendous stone structures throughout the world are classified as "unattributed," meaning nobody really knows who built them, and they generally resemble each other in construction as well as alignment to planets, the sun and moon and their orbits, to the constellations and other fixed stars, and to other forces as well, possibly the magnetic fields and currents of the earth. These enigmatical prehistoric structures include the pyramids of Teotihuacán in Mexico and the older cities of Yucatán, the pre-Inca ruins of the Peruvian Andes and the lines of the Nasca Valley, the massive ruins of Tiahuanaco at an altitude of 13,500 feet, the giant stone structures of the British Isles, especially Stonehenge and Avebury, and the great standing stones of Brittany, some of which continue out under the ocean, the prehistoric ruins on the islands of the Mediterranean, in the Middle East, and Southeast Asia, the cyclopean remains on the Carolines, Marquesas, and other islands in the Pacific, the monolithic structures under the Caribbean, the prehistoric stonework of Niebla, in Spain, and the unattributed works of North Africa, including Egypt, the alignment of the great mounds of the United States, and the archaic pyramids of China.

Until the first decade of the present century, all dwellings in China, before they were built, were oriented by a necromancer in order to take advantage of the felicitous paths or unseen currents running across and through the earth. (It will be remembered that the first compasses, as we know them, came from China.) A perceptive commentator on the landscape architecture of China, Dr. Ernst Börschmann, thought the arrangement of temples, pagodas, and pavilions, aligned to a center from which they radiated, resembled a magnetic field. The procedure of following force lines in the earth (in Chinese *feng shui*—"wind-water"), possibly a hold-over from an advanced ancient science, has now been dropped as being superstitious and feudalistic although another form of superstition, acupuncture, which itself may be another scientifically valid relic disguised through the centuries as magic, has been elevated to a position of respectability by the present regime in China.

If the force of magnetism and reverse magnetism had been understood and developed in very ancient times to a point where gravity, in itself a form of magnetism, could be channeled like other natural forces, an explanation might be at hand for some of the technologically impossible prehistoric constructions, many of which seem to have literally been thrown up to the tops of mountains and perched on the edges of precipices as if these monolithic stones had flown there.

It is intriguing to reflect that some residue of ancient electromagnetic techniques may still be protecting the Egyptian pyramids while the scientists of today are endeavoring to reveal their secrets—in this case sealed chambers within the pyramids. For some time there has been a project under way to penetrate the inner structure of the Chephren Pyramid at Gîza by recording penetration by cosmic rays of the stones' mass. This project has been under the direction of Dr. Amr Gohed, of the University of Ein Shams, Cairo, using, among other equipment, a new IBM 1130 computer. Although the tests were expertly applied, the recordings, day after day, have given completely different recorded patterns in the same areas. According to Dr. Gohed: ". . . It defies all the known laws of science and electronics . . ." and is "scientifically impossible." A London *Times* article reported that: ". . . The hopes of a great discovery were now found to be a mass of meaningless symbols . . ." and Dr. Gohed, in assessing the up to now failure of the project, said: ". . . There is some influence that defies the laws of science at work in the pyramid . . ."

Rather than being a defiance of the laws of science, what may be concerned here could simply be other laws or use or modification of other laws that we do not understand even today—stresses and pulls that represent the hidden forces of the earth, the planets, the sun, the moon, and the stars.

In his book *The View Over Atlantis,* John Mitchell refers to the unity of prehistoric culture and observes that: ". . . The earth is strewn with works of prehistoric engineering connected with the use of polar magnetism." He suggests that we live: ". . . within the ruins of an ancient structure whose vast size has hitherto rendered it invisible . . ."—linking together the great stone remains of prehistory still standing on the plains, mountains, deserts, in the jungles, and under the seas of the world. In his opinion: ". . . the philosophers of that time [considered that] the earth was a living creature and its body, like that of every other creature, had a nervous system within and relating to its magnetic field. The nerve centers of the earth, corresponding on the human body to the acupuncture points of Chinese medicine, were guarded and sanctified by sacred building, themselves laid out as microcosms of the cosmic order . . ."

Indications that there may have been one or more world civilizations in the remote past that disappeared as a result of natural or self-induced catastrophes which happened considerably prior to our own recorded cultural beginnings in the fourth millennium B.C. have largely survived as fragments of advanced knowledge, retold or recopied through the centuries. Buildings or monuments that may have come down from such a period, imposing as they are, are difficult or impossible to date. In addition, the extent of the time slot which we have previously reserved for the appearance and development of civilized man scarcely permits the time needed for the building of this largely hypothetical culture. However, the recent discoveries by Dr. Louis Leakey and Mary Leakey in Olduvai Gorge, Tanzania, and those of Richard Leakey in Kenya, indicate that primitive man may go back as far as 2,000,000 years, and findings in the Vallonet caves in France have dated primitive tools as 1,000,000 years old. The study of the skulls of Cro-Magnon man (generally considered to have existed 30,000 to 35,000 years before our era) indicates that his skull capacity, with its inferred brain size, was at least equal to and sometimes superior to our own.

While the marvelous cave paintings of animals in France and Spain, often located in caves which have fallen beneath ground level, have been accepted as part of the world's heritage of art, other less-known artistic records may eventually cause a basic re-evaluation of the age of civilized man. Pictures scratched on flat pieces of rock, dated by layers of covering earth, at Lussac-les-Châteaux, France, show such surprising drawings of the period usually associated with cavemen as to be almost incredible; at a time thousands of years before the dawn of civilization as we know it, unexpectedly modern-appearing people are shown wearing robes, boots, belts, coats, and hats, and men are shown with clipped beards and mustaches.

Other sophisticated wall paintings deep within caves in South Africa, of approximately the same period, depict white travelers, wearing elaborate but unidentifiable garments, engaged in what may have been a prehistoric safari or voyage of exploration.

Concepts of prehistoric evolution postulate that one type of man follows another on the ascending evolutionary scale, with the best-fitted and most highly developed types replacing the more primitive. While this is generally true, with the advanced Cro-Magnon type replacing the brutish Neanderthal man, it was still possible during Earth's long history for both these types, and others as well, to coexist, a situation we find existing even today in a world population which includes atomic scientists and Australian aborigines.

If an advanced civilization did exist before those we know of, it seems reasonable to expect that some indication would survive, furnishing a clear proof (if anything is ever completely clear in archaeological research) that such a technically developed culture existed not just several but many thousands of years ago. However, just as would be the case with our own civilization were it to be destroyed, most of the buildings, machines, and artifacts would decay, rust, scatter, and become unrecognizable before several thousand years had gone by. Some indications might conceivably survive if they were buried within the shifting earth, under the permafrost of the North or the Antarctic ice, or hidden on the bottom of the sea.

The development of the carbon 14, potassium argon, uranium thorium, thermoluminescence, dendrochronology (tree-ring dating), and other dating processes has shaken some of our long held theories about the first dates of civilization. An iron mine in Ngwenya, Lesotho, was worked by unknown miners 43,000 years ago. Stone tools found in Iran have been given a date of

100,000 years. Large-scale copper-mining operations in northern Michigan apparently predated the Indians by thousands of years. In Wattis, Utah, a new tunnel dug into a coal mine broke into an unsuspected series of existing tunnels of unknown age. The coal found in these tunnels was so weathered that it was useless for burning. There were no Indian legends concerning such mines, nor did Indians use tunnel techniques for mining.

As man has explored deeper within the earth, certain tooled artifacts have been discovered contained within coal, stone, or other strata, implying an age so great that it can be only roughly calculated. A shoe print in Fisher Canyon, Nevada, embedded within a coal seam, has been estimated as being 15,000,000 years old; a print of a ribbed sole of a shoe or sandal found in sandstone rock under the Gobi Desert is thought to have been made several million years ago. Still another fossilized footprint of a sandal, uncovered in the vicinity of Delta, Utah, contained trilobites embedded in it, meaning that they came after the sandal print or were attached to it. Trilobites were Paleozoic marine animals that have been extinct, it is believed, for at least 200,000,000 years. A fossilized human skeleton excavated from a mine in Italy in 1959 was surrounded by strata whose age was calculated in millions of years.

A piece of quartz found in California revealed that there was an iron nail inside it, completely encompassed, like the prehistoric insects preserved in amber in the North Sea. A piece of feldspar from the Abbey Mine in Treasure City, Nevada, in 1865, was found to contain a two-inch metal screw, which had oxidized but left its form and the shape of its threads *within* the feldspar; the stone itself was calculated as being millions of years old. In the last century at the village of

Schöndorf, near Vöcklabruck, Austria, a small iron cubelike object, less than a centimeter in length and breadth, was discovered inside a block of coal which had been split open. An incised line forms a groove around the cube, which has rounded edges, as if machine-tooled. There is, of course, no explanation as to what it was or how it got inside the block of coal millions of years ago.

At the time of the conquest of Peru there is a record that a nail was found within a rock by a Spanish-directed Indian crew within a Peruvian mine, an incident which caused consternation not only because of its apparent age but because iron was unknown in America before the arrival of the Spaniards.

A mastodon found at Blue Lick Springs in Kentucky was excavated at a depth of twelve feet. But, as digging continued, a cut-and-set-stone pavement was found three feet deeper, *under* where the mastodon had been lying. This is only one instance of finds of ancient stonework within the United States, so old that its dating by surrounding or superadjacent objects (as in the case of the mastodon) has not been accepted.

These and other cases are so difficult to explain in terms of history that many are inclined to disbelieve them entirely while others credit them to visitors from other worlds who left their footprints on our world at eras so remote that what is now solid rock were malleable and viscous areas. The possibility exists, however, that these footprints and simple objects were made by men of extremely ancient races living on the earth and that the discoveries in mines mean that this civilization was so far back in time that only what has been hidden within the earth or preserved within other materials has so far been found, and even then not identified. One wonders how many small clues have been destroyed throughout the centuries with only a few enigmas remaining to furnish any evidence of predawn civilization other than legends.

Legends and carved pictorial representations of extinct but recognizable animals may be another indication of the antiquity of human culture. An animal closely resembling the toxodon is depicted on pottery found at Tiahuanaco, the two-and-a-half-mile-high city in the Andes of Bolivia. The toxodon, a prehistoric animal somewhat like the hippopotamus, had previously been considered to be extinct long before the development of civilized man and, in any case, his habitat was not adapted to a barren 13,500-foot-high plateau such as Tiahuanaco, nor would the Tiahuanaco area have been a likely spot for the site of a great culture, and there are indications, such as cornfield terraces above the present snow line in the surrounding mountains and a deep lake containing oceanic fauna, that the entire area may have been thousands of feet lower when Tiahuanaco was built, perhaps at sea level and on the coast.

On the Marcahuasi Plateau near Kenko, Peru, there are tremendous rock carvings—in some cases whole cliffs are modified by carving. These pre-Inca carvings, although weathered by countless ages, can be identified as lions, horses, camels, and elephants, none of which are supposed to have lived in South America during the time of civilized man. Also in Peru, llamas drawn on very ancient pre-Inca pottery found in the ruins of a coastal city near Pisco, are shown with five toes, as they once had many thousands of years ago, instead of the cloven hoof they later developed.

What appear to be dinosaurs have been discovered

in petroglyphs incised on rock formations in both North and South America. But since ordinary lizards, gila monsters, and iguanas, for example, resembled their remote dinosaur ancestors, it is difficult to determine whether these examples represent prehistoric monsters or ordinary lizards. This may be the case with an Indian or pre-Indian pictograph depicting a great lizard, scratched on a rock formation on Big Sandy River, Oregon. The picture, however, is an excellent likeness of a stegosaur.

The Doheny Expedition in 1924 found petroglyphs of extreme age in the Havasupai Canyon near the Grand Canyon. One stone picture showed men attacking a mammoth, an unexpected petroglyph to be found in America, where man has usually been considered, geologically speaking, a fairly recent arrival. Among other pictographs examined there was a reasonably accurate portrayal of a tyrannosaur, standing upright, partly supporting himself on his tail, exactly as later museum reproductions have shown him. Other petroglyphs along the Amazon and its tributaries show what seem to be other prehistoric animals, especially the stegosaur.

Near the village of Acámbaro, Mexico, during the excavation of a site in 1945, clay statuettes were unearthed which have been the cause of an archaeological uproar through the years. They consist of models of rhinoceroses, camels, horses, giant monkeys, as well as dinosaurs of the Mesozoic era. (The find was further discredited since the discoverer, Waldemar Julsrud, offering to pay only for whole statuettes found, inadvertently encouraged reproductions to be made by the local Indians.) Carbon 14 tests on the figurines, however, indicate that they are from 3,000 to 6,500 years old. One of the figures so closely resembles a dinosaur called the brachiosaur that, were it not for the geological eras in between, one would believe that the artist had actually seen such an animal.

The fact that early man drew or modeled animals that resembled dinosaurs is, of course, no proof that he ever saw them (although he could have seen their bones). The dragon of St. George and the dragon of China, as well as the dragon-like sirrush, portrayed among real animals along the walls of Babylon, were scarcely physical realities. Nevertheless, certain details suggest that early man may have appeared much sooner than is commonly believed and that he dealt with some animals supposed to be extinct at his point in time.

Some of these survivors would be located in time in the later epochs of the Tertiary era. However, since some of the pictographs seem to portray reptiles of the Mesozoic era, long before the advent of man, one might suggest an intriguing explanation. If highly civilized man existed on earth in an epoch before ours, his scientific curiosity would have led him to the discovery of the former presence of the Jurassic dinosaurs as has been the case with us. With the disappearance of this former civilization this knowledge might have been preserved through legends (of dragons) and pictographs. Again, as in the case of our own civilization, one must remember that little more than 100 years ago traditionalists explained the presence of enormous fossils in the earth by claming that God had made the fossils at the same time he created the earth.

Andrew Tomas, writing of historic anachronisms in his book *We Are Not the First,* tells of an excavated skull of an auroch (an ancient wild ox) now in the Paleontological museum in Moscow. The skull, several hundred thousand years old, is pierced on the frontal part by a small hole evidently caused by a round projectile. The lack of radial split lines, the speed and heat of the projectile, as well as its shape, suggest a bullet. The supposed bullet was not fired after the auroch's death, since investigation showed that the wound had healed some time after it was inflicted. There is another such example in London (The Museum of Natural History), where there is on display a human skull, found in a cave in Zambia, and dated as 40,000 years old, with a comparable hole on the left side, also without radial cracks. The possibilities implied by these prehistoric shootings, if such they are, are intriguing.

These discoveries, isolated and interpretive though they may be, point to the probability that civilized man has existed on Earth much longer than was previously assumed. Without even considering the possibility of civilization being brought to Earth from outer space, as has been frequently suggested, there would be time and space in the history of our own planet for one or several cultures to have developed to the point of annihilating themselves through warfare, disturbance of the environment, or of being destroyed by other forces which they may have unconsciously triggered.

Our own culture, if we assume a starting point of 4000 B.C., has progressed from primitive agriculture and herding to nuclear fission in only 6,000 years. Considering the age of mankind, there has been ample time for other cultures to have arrived at a level roughly corresponding to ours. A re-examination of some of the ancient records that have come down to us might give some indication of mankind having previously attained our present aptitude for destruction. While there are hints of great blastings of the earth's surface in the Bible (Sodom and Gomorrah), the Greek myths, and many of the legends of the Indians of North and South America, it is in the ancient records of India, copied and recopied from prehistoric antiquity, that we find, described in considerable detail, the use and effect of what closely resembles atomic explosions in warfare.

Unexpected references to such recent developments of our technological civilization are present in many of the ancient books of India, which, unlike so many records of the Western world, escaped burning and destruction. These references deal, almost as if they were written today instead of thousands of years ago, with such matters as the relativity of time and space, cosmic rays, the law of gravity, radiation, the kinetic nature of energy, and the atomic theory. The Vaisesika school of science philosophers of ancient India developed or preserved the theory that atoms were in incessant motion. They subdivided the measure of time into a series of incredible fractions of seconds, the most infinitesimal being considered as the "period taken by an atom to traverse its own unit of space."

Surprisingly modern-sounding references abound in the *Mahabharata,* a gigantic compendium of over 200,000 verses dealing with the creation of the cosmos, religion, prayers, customs, history, and legends about the gods and heroes of ancient India. It is supposed to have been originally written 3,500 years ago, but it refers to events that reputedly took place thousands of years before that. Among the verses of the *Mahabharata,* there are a number that contain vivid descriptions of what seem to be a firsthand view of atomic warfare.

When Western students of philosophy and religion,

in the 1880s, were able to read and study the *Maha-bharata* (a translation had been completed in 1884), they naturally considered as poetic fancy the frequent and curiously detailed references to ancient airships (*vimanas*), with instructions of how they were powered and how to recognize enemy aircraft. There were even more puzzling references to a weapon to paralyze enemy armies (*mohanastra*—"the arrow of uncon-sciousness"), as well as descriptions of "two-storey sky chariots with many windows ejecting red flame that race up into the sky until they look like comets . . . to the regions of both the sun and the stars."

It must be remembered that the *Mahabharata* was translated decades before the appearance of aircraft, poison or nerve gas, manned rockets, and atomic bombs. Such references signified nothing other than wild flights of the imagination to readers of the Vic-torian era. Other references were easily understood by occidental students of the *Mahabharata* inasmuch as they referred to relatively modern weaponry and con-cerned controlled fire power, different kinds of artillery and rockets, "bullets of iron," lead shot, explosives of saltpeter, sulphur, and charcoal, rocket bombs capable of reducing city gates, and the *agneyastras,* cylindrical cannons which made a noise like thunder. Even though these were attributed to ancient India, they failed to amaze the readers, some of whom suspected that they were "intrusive" or slipped in between the translation in an understandable Indian attempt to say "we had them before you."

Other mysterious weapons mentioned in the *Maha-bharata* were better understood, although they had been fairly incomprehensible before, during the development of World War I. An Indian military commentator,

Ramchandra Dikshitar (*War in Ancient India*), pointed out that warfare had caught up with the *Mahabharata* with modern airplanes being the equivalent of *vimanas,* the *mohanastra* weapon which caused armies to fall unconscious being the equivalent to poison gas; he also pointed out the use of the fog dart which produced a dense camouflage fog and compared the *tashtra,* "capable of slaying large numbers of foes together" with improved modern explosives. While scholars of the last century and some British officers of World War I could recognize some of the "rediscovered" weapons of the *Mahabharata,* other descriptions were so inconceivable that they confused the translators. Even the principal translator, P. Chandra Roy, observed in the introduction: "To the purely English reader there is much in this book that will strike him as ridiculous."

What was mysterious or ridiculous in the 1880s and even during World War I, however, is no longer enigmatical to almost anyone alive in today's uncertain world. The following excerpts, dealing with an ancient war, are chillingly familiar to us, although separated from our own atomic era by thousands of years. A description of a special weapon launched against an opposing army goes as follows:

A single projectile charged with all the power of the Universe. An incandescent column of smoke and flame, as bright as ten thousand Suns, rose in all its splendor. . . . it was an unknown weapon, an iron thunderbolt, a gigantic messenger of death which reduced to ashes the entire race of the Vrishnis and the Andhakas [the enemies it was used against]. . . . The corpses were so burned as to be unrecognizable. Their hair and nails fell out; pottery broke without any apparent cause, and the birds turned white.

After a few hours, all foodstuffs were infected. . . .
to escape from this fire, the soldiers threw themselves
in streams to wash themselves and all their equipment. . . .

[That mighty weapon] . . . bore away crowds [of
warriors] with steeds and elephants and cars and
weapons as if these were dry leaves of trees . . . borne
away by the wind . . . they looked highly beautiful
like flying birds . . . flying away from trees . . .

Instead of referring to the subsequent visual results
after the explosion of such a superweapon as the mush-
room cloud, the writer, who saw, compiled from other
accounts, or simply imagined the effect, described it as
great clouds opening one over the other like a series of
several gigantic parasols: a different notion than ours,
but not at all a bad simile.

Even the approximate measurements of the weapon
or bomb are given:

. . . A shaft fatal as the rod of death. It measured
three cubits and six feet. Endowed with the force
of thousand-eyed Indra's thunder, it was . . . destructive of all living creatures. . . .

An account is recorded of the meeting of two missiles
in the air.

. . . The two weapons met each other in mid air.
Then earth with all her mountains and seas and trees
began to tremble, and all living creatures were heated
with the energy of the weapons and greatly affected.
The skies blazed and the ten points of the horizon
became filled with smoke. . . .

The great war described in the *Mahabharata* is thought by many to refer to the "Aryan" invasion of the Indian subcontinent from the north, a narrative that could have been described in understandable terms, in proportion to the era, as was the *Iliad,* without recourse to such science fiction and strangely prophetic type weapons.

It is pertinent to point out, however, that skeletons discovered in the extremely ancient cities of Mohenjo-Daro and Harappa, Pakistan, have been found to be extremely radioactive. Practically nothing is known of the histories of these very ancient cities except that they were suddenly destroyed.

Ancient descriptions of airplanes and atomic warfare of course do not necessarily mean, however prescient they may prove, that the writer witnessed such marvels personally or that they ever existed except in his active or febrile imagination. In our own era the Buck Rogers comic strip was freely dealing with the use of atomic bombs until the FBI, shortly before the supersecret real atomic bomb was tested in New Mexico, persuaded the author to desist from such references in his strip. Another unwitting prophetic coincidence of a science fiction nature was contained in Jules Verne's *Voyage à la Lune,* when he established Florida as a base for his fictional moon shot, upstaging the real moon shot by more than a century. By a further prophetic coincidence, the measurements given by Verne, 100 years ago, for Captain Nemo's imaginary submarine are almost identical with those of the present U.S. atomic subs. Even more mystifying was the case of Swift and the moons of Mars. In writing *Gulliver's Travels* in 1726, Swift described the satellites of Mars and gave their approximately correct measurements and particulars of their revolution around the planet, despite the fact that the two moons he so casually (and exactly) referred to in a fictional work were not even discovered until 1877. Nevertheless, Verne, Swift, and the creator of Buck Rogers were living in a scientific age wherein the possibility of such discoveries or inventions was simply a matter of time. But the Indian records stem from perhaps more than six thousand years ago.

Certain Asians, and Westerners as well, who subscribe to the theory that civilized man has existed for a much longer time than previously suspected (and the pushing back of the time curtain of civilization does indeed seem to leave centuries and even millennia which may yet be filled in) do not find unbelievable the possibility of cresting and vanishing waves of civilization throughout the world, some of which have left no trace except in legend. They therefore are prepared to believe that the unexpectedly detailed Indian references to atoms, atomic structure, atomic weapons, and advanced technology may be simply a preserved memory of prehistoric and scientifically advanced civilizations.

In the legends of India, we should also consider the fact that certain sections of the earth's surface seem to show atomic scars acquired millennia previous to present atomic activities. These locations exist in Siberia, Iraq, Colorado, and Mongolia (where Chinese atomic tests are leaving new scars comparable to the ancient ones and, in some places, considerably below the present ground level).

In the course of an exploratory digging in southern Iraq in 1947, layers of culture were successively cored into by what one might call an archaeological mine shaft. Starting from the present ground level, the excavation passed the ancient city culture levels of Babylonia, Chaldea, and Sumeria, with flood levels between different ages of city culture, then the first village levels, then a level corresponding to that of primitive farmers at a time era of 6000 to 7000 B.C., and below that, indications of a herdsman culture, and finally a time era was reached corresponding to the Magdalenian or cave culture of about 16,000 years ago. Still farther down, at the bottom of all levels, a floor of fused glass was revealed, similar to nothing else except the desert floor in New Mexico after the blasts which inaugurated our present atomic era.

9

The Watchers:
Protectors, Raiders, or
Indifferent Observers

IF PLANES, SHIPS, AND PEOPLE ARE BEING KIDNAPED,
especially from the Bermuda Triangle, and from
other areas of the world, by UFOs or other means, an
important factor of any investigation should be the
consideration of a possible reason or reasons. Some
researchers have suggested that intelligent entities, light-
years scientifically advanced over the comparatively
primitive peoples of the earth, have been engaged
throughout the centuries in observing our progress and
will eventually intervene to prevent us from destroying
our own planet. This would, of course, presume the
existence of an altruistic nature on the part of beings
from inner or outer space, a feature not always dominant among explorers or pioneers.

On the other hand, it may be that there exists, in
the vicinity of the Bermuda Triangle and certain other
nodal locations of electromagnetic gravitational currents, a door or window to another dimension in time

or space through which extraterrestrials sufficiently sophisticated scientifically can penetrate at will but which, when encountered by humans, would represent a one-way street from which return would either be impossible to their level of scientific advancement or would be barred by alien force. Many of the disappearances, especially those concerning entire ship's crews, suggest raiding expeditions, ranging from collecting human beings for space zoos, for exhibits of different eras in planetary development, or for experimentation.

Dr. Manson Valentine suggests that there may be various and sometimes inimical groups of space visitors and that some of these visiting entities, coming from space, the oceanic depths, or even another dimension, may be related to us—our own cousins of many thousands of years ago, sufficiently civilized to have an altruistic reason for protecting us and the earth, or pragmatically concerned for their own environment.

From this latter point of view it is evident that Earth and its populations are in increasingly greater danger of planet-wide ruin and destruction. This situation may already have happened on several occasions in past millennia, but although the earth was in danger, it was not made uninhabitable as may have been the fate of several nearby planets and moons. Memories of near fatal world catastrophes are still preserved among certain ancient races that have all but disappeared. According to the traditions of several ancient races, there has not been only one global catastrophe but several. The Indian races of Middle America have counted three world endings until now and are counting on a fourth ending of the world—this time by fire—at a date not too far in the future. The Hopi, who, among the Indian tribes in the United States, preserve the most complete and oddly detailed record of their wanderings and of the cosmos itself, also tell of three previous endings of the world, once by volcanic eruption and fire, once by earthquakes and the temporary spinning of the world off its axis, and a third time by inundations and sinking of the continents because the warlike inhabitants of the "Third World" were destroying each other's cities by aerial warfare. Parenthetically, the reference to the earth spinning off its axis is itself an indication of extraordinary knowledge held by a small Indian tribe, not only of the true shape of the earth, but of its rotation. The theory of the earth losing its spin and then readjusting is in accord with a later scientific theory developed by Hugh Auchincloss Brown, who predicates the disturbance of spin to a developing overweight of ice on one of the poles.

Ancient religious legends of India tell of nine crises of the world, while other cultures of antiquity vary somewhat concerning the number, although not the recurring frequency of global catastrophes.

Plato, in his dialogue *Critias,* quotes an Egyptian priest telling the Athenian lawgiver Solon, who was on a visit to Egypt:

> . . . There have been, and there will be again, many destructions of mankind arising out of many causes.

After explaining to Solon how the Egyptians, because of their records, had maintained memories of some of these events, he allegedly observed to Solon:

> . . . and then, at the usual period, the stream from heaven descends like a pestilence . . . and thus you have to begin all over again as children. . . . [adding, as a final thrust at the lack of Greek records] You

remember one deluge only, whereas there were many of them. . . .

The cyclic theory of civilization, prevalent in the ancient world and still, to a certain extent, in Asia, is in marked contrast to the progress theory of our own culture, with its preoccupation with the passage and pressure of time, and the constantly forward march of civilization and scientific development. As our own knowledge increases, however, we may find that what was suspected by observers in antiquity will be shown to have eventually transpired.

World catastrophes and destructions of entire civilizations may have previously resulted from a variety of causes, several of which face us today, however resolutely we may refuse to contemplate them. Outstanding among these is the question of overpopulation, a problem about which one finds mention in the records of antiquity only in the *Mahabharata,* as if the Indian subcontinent had suffered then as now from strangling overpopulation. Nuclear warfare, suggested by the records of antiquity and another outstanding dilemma of today, is, of course, one way of inadvertently solving the overpopulation problem, although it carries with it the problem of destroying much of the life on the planet and even damaging its future habitability as well as, if the atomic reactions are strong enough, causing seismic disasters and eventually floods from the melting icecaps.

Other catastrophes may be presently developing even now, unconnected with atomic activity but linked to technological development, the results of which will only be known with the passage of time. For today, besides our atomic tests, nuclear waste, environmental pollution of air and water, and unbalancing of the ecology, we are unwittingly engaged in several gradual experiments which may eventually have startling consequences.

An example of the above may be suggested by the observation of Dr. Columbus Islin, former director of Woods Hole Oceanographic Institution. Discussing the increase of carbon dioxide in the atmosphere, he states:

> During the last 100 years, the increasing use of fossil fuels in our world-wide industrial civilization should result in the production of about 1,700 billion tons of carbon dioxide, 70 per cent of the amount now in the atmosphere. Because about two-thirds of the added carbon dioxide is absorbed by the sea, an increase of perhaps 20 per cent in atmospheric carbon dioxide can be expected.
>
> The effect of such an increase is not easy to predict, but there is reason to believe that it could result in the warming of the lower atmosphere by several degrees. Thus, we are conducting more or less in spite of ourselves a great experiment.

The effect of a man-inspired melting of the polar ice together with tidal waves and flooding of seacoasts throughout the world is reminiscent of what we now consider to be the far from legendary Flood of prehistory which covered surface lands in the Atlantic, the Caribbean, the Mediterranean, and elsewhere. Even the spillage of oil from one of the increasingly huge supertankers or from an Arctic pipeline might begin a large-scale melting of polar ice with unpredictable effects.

The extinction of so many species of animal life may be another potential source of future disaster about which we cannot yet form an opinion. In a previous catastrophe, it will be remembered that Noah, an ecologist before it became fashionable, while he took seven pairs of each of the more useful animals aboard the Ark, also took one pair of each of all the other animals, whether they were useful or not. Perhaps the climb from barbarism to civilization and eventually knowledge and ability to use nuclear fission is, in the case of man and other intelligences equally equipped, a natural process and has taken place before not only on Earth but in other parts of the universe. Perhaps other civilized systems, extraterrestrial or even, as suggested by Valentine, Sanderson, and others, of this same Earth, although not apparent to us, have triumphed over this urge for self-destruction and are studying our world through such paths or open doors as the Bermuda Triangle, either as an object lesson or to preserve parts of its culture for study, or to keep it from destroying itself. Perhaps they even plan to guide it, as stronger nations attempt to do with the less developed ones. But to ascribe motives to such observers would be to assume that they think as we do: wild animals cannot possibly understand why collectors want to trap and exhibit them instead of killing and eating them. Possibly, as has been suggested, the UFOs are simply "scouting" our planet. If so, they have been at it for an exceedingly long time.

If there is any truth in the hypothesis that alien entities are visiting and observing Earth and collecting information and samples for whatever purpose, especially within the area of the Bermuda Triangle, it is interesting to speculate why this area should be one of special UFO concentration. Sightings of "heavenly" aircraft in the distant past suggest that they have appeared in areas of cultural and technical development at certain points of apogee as if to ascertain, from time to time, where new centers of civilization were developing and whether or not they were potentially dangerous. We have only to note the sequence of ancient reports relating to heavenly visits to Earth by gods or aircraft to discern a vague pattern of shifting emphasis. The first visits described in detail were those to ancient Egypt at the time of Thutmose III and the space trip undertaken by the Sumerian Etana. We have, of course, more detailed indications of extraterrestrial contact in the Book of Ezekiel, who related visits to Earth by what appear to be spacecraft on four occasions within nineteen years, and who on one occasion saw two of them and, like Etana, was himself a passenger; as well as a possible indication in the case of Elijah, who ascended to the heavens in a "fiery chariot"—never to return. From India we have a memory of space flight in the description of the flight of Rama and in ancient American references to gods who came in machines from the sky to build Tiahuanaco. Successively, the many reports from Greece, Rome, Renaissance Europe, and, in our day, an increasing number from all over the world, but especially from the Bermuda Triangle, suggest the possibility that the observers seem to be interested in the advance of technological civilization on the earth, especially as regards air travel, space penetration, and modern warfare. In World War II and the Korean War a number of "foo fighters" (unidentified lights or objects accompanying bomber or fighter planes in flight) were fairly commonplace, while reported concentrations of UFOs at present seem to be in the vicinity of space-travel areas, either because they represent a development of technological potential or a threat to the solar system or part of the universe.

The theories of Ivan Sanderson, however, suggest that the increasing threat to our own ocean environment may be shared by highly developed life forms within the ocean.

There appear to have been several startling confirmations (in addition to the instances listed in Chapter 6) of UFO *undersea* activity having been observed and tracked by U. S. Navy units. These incidents have, as is customary, been "depublicized" as much as possible except for the initial reports. One of the most striking concerns the tracking of an underwater object, moving at over 150 knots, first by a destroyer and subsequently by a submarine during a U. S. Navy exercise southeast of Puerto Rico in 1963, at the southern edge of the Bermuda Triangle. As the maneuver was effectively a drill in tracking, it was assumed that the object was part of the exercise and thirteen other Navy craft noted the rapidly moving propelled object and entered the report in their ship's log. It was tracked for a total of four days, at times penetrating depths of 27,000 feet while maintaining its incredible speed. It was never ascertained what it was, although most reports agreed that it appeared to be powered by a single propeller.

While reports of UFOs emerging from, descending into, or operating within the seas have been fairly prevalent in the past, seldom have they been so closely detected and tracked as in the 1963 maneuvers just described.

Supposing the existence of an older branch of humanity or other "civilized" life form under the seas, such entities, with a vastly greater amount of living space at their disposal than that tenuously held by surface-dwelling civilized life forms such as ourselves, would not have concerned themselves with our actions during the last several millennia. But once our technical potential represented a danger to them and to their environment, their *laissez-faire* policy might well change and the Bermuda Triangle phenomena may be a tentative preview or exploratory action prior to something more definitive.

Ivan Sanderson suggested that certain unexplained and unpublicized reports of giant undersea transparent domes, some of which had been seen by sponge divers off the coast of Spain and also glimpsed from the surface, when underwater visibility was favorable, by lobster fishermen and commercial fishermen on the American continental shelf, might be (if not secret defense installations) parts of an undersea grid being constructed by undersea terrestrials for purposes possibly connected with neutralizing the ongoing pollution and poisoning of the sea. Extending this train of thought still further, it would conceivably be possible, as the earth is essentially an enormous dynamo, to "wire" the earth by laying electromagnetic networks within the oceans and, eventually, by activating the proper impulses to change the rotation of the earth.

This tapping of the earth itself is reminiscent of ancient traditions as well as comparatively new theories regarding the great power sources of Atlantis, the crystal laser complexes which may lie on the floor of the Sargasso Sea, still partially functioning after thousands of years and intermittently causing electromagnetic stresses or drains resulting in the malfunction or disintegration of sea and air craft.

It is, of course, natural for us to speculate about the reasons for the visits of extraterrestrial beings and to seek to identify their purposes within our own frame of reference. Following this reasoning, it is normal to suppose that the visitors have come to protect us from ourselves, while other less sanguine observers have presumed that the visitors have come not for the purpose of protection but rather for collection. The latter supposition would seem more logical considering the number of planes, boats, and ships and their crews that have vanished within the Bermuda Triangle.

Dr. John Harder, Professor of Engineering at Berkeley, and investigator of UFOs, recently (October 1973) expressed the unusual though scarcely flattering theory that the earth may be a sort of "cosmic zoo, shut off from the rest of the universe and every so often the keepers make a random sample check of the inhabitants."

But another suggested theory implies that the visitors are indifferent to humanity, being occupied with their own aims, which as yet we are unable to imagine, and that the apparent casualties (since we still do not definitely know if anyone has died in the disappearances) have been caused *inadvertently,* by projection into the field of ionization.

This theory has long furnished newspaper and magazine writers with periodic opportunities for titles such as "Lost Atlantis is Alive and Well and Kidnapping Ships and Planes." The concept that a laser beam can destroy or atomize a plane is possible but the idea that power installations or gigantic laser complexes could still function after thousands of years' immersion in the sea seems patently ridiculous, as giant lasers, as we conceive them, would have to be maintained and operated.

However, lasers are a comparatively recent development in our world and it is probable that they will be brought to a much higher degree of perfection in the future. The ultraviolet laser (not yet developed) will have considerably more energy than the X-ray lasers, as will also be the case when lasers operate from stored solar power or presumably, in the instance of Atlantis, power from *inside* the earth. In any event, a highly civilized technological era of the past would not necessarily develop in the same way or in the same order as our own, nor would it be subject to the same restrictions which presently and temporarily limit our still developing technology.

In considering the hundreds of disappearances in the Bermuda Triangle, one notes that the single common thread which unites them is the fact that the ships and planes have completely vanished or that the ships have been found without their crews and passengers. While isolated mysteries of this nature could be explained by unusual circumstances or coincidences of weather and human error, so many of the Bermuda Triangle incidents have happened in clear weather, near to port, shore, or landing base, that they seem unexplainable according to our presently held concepts.

The history of the Bermuda Triangle encompasses events clouded by the mists of ancient and modern legend, the unexplained and apparently intermittent aberrations of natural forces, and theories of physics as yet unproved which could revolutionize our previously held concepts. The Bermuda Triangle leads back to lost and sunken lands, to forgotten civilizations, to visitors to the earth through the centuries from outer or inner space whose provenance and purpose are unknown.

Rather than theorize about explaining the presently

unexplainable, it is perhaps easier to say that the Bermuda Triangle exists only in the imagination of mystics, cultists, the superstitious and the sensational-minded. One of the several commentators who believes that the Bermuda Triangle is nothing more than a coincidence of disappearances, each of which can be separately explained, has observed, "Those who believe in the Bermuda Triangle also believe in sea serpents," although the latter epigram is not necessarily a proof that if one does not exist the other does not either, or that, if a sea serpent is finally and satisfactorily identified, then other legends of the sea automatically become more credible.

In general, people are unwilling to confront mysteries which cannot be eventually explained or incapable of theoretical explanation in terms they can understand. It is more spiritually comforting to be able to recognize what we may face on the perimeter of the physical world than to face an unknown threat. If the phenomenon cannot be explained, the best response is to ignore it—a more reassuring course of action and, in a way, more innocent. But the time of scientific innocence, together with its implied reassurance, has passed, having definitely ended on the morning of July 16, 1945, at Alamogordo, New Mexico, when the atomic theory established its own conclusive proof that it was no longer a theory.

We now live in a world where the lines of science and parascience are converging—a world where what was once magic or the dreams of magicians has been adopted by science and made acceptable by scientific nomenclature. Biologists can now produce life; cryogenic biologists will soon be able to preserve human life indefinitely through freezing live bodies; thought transference of pictures to film has been proven; psychokinesis, the moving of objects by force of will, is no longer a matter for levity but one for serious experimentation; telepathy to and from outer space is the subject for experiments by both of the leading space powers. The alchemists' dream, the transmutation of matter, is no longer an impossibility, and the only impediment to transmuting quantities of lead into gold is that it would be too expensive(!).

On a more cosmic scale the firmament of scientific verities has opened into crevices so great that many of those who prefer to stand on solid and familiar ground feel dizzy and disoriented. The possibility of the existence of antimatter, the curvature of space and time, new concepts of gravity and magnetism, the suspected existence of dark planets in our own system, imploding suns, novas and small particles of matter heavier than an entire planet, quasars and the dark holes in space, an endless universe which grows larger as our telescopic vision extends to millions of undiscovered galaxies—this is the arcane knowledge that awaits us as we rush forward at so accelerated a speed that no "mystery" should surprise us simply because it does not seem logical.

The Bermuda Triangle, an area located on the familiar territory of our planet, although perhaps connected with forces which we do not yet (but may soon) understand, may be one of these mysteries. As a species, we are now approaching maturity. We cannot retreat from the search for knowledge or new explanations—either in this world or beyond.

Acknowledgments

THE AUTHOR WISHES TO EXPRESS HIS APPRECIATION to the following persons and organizations who have contributed advice, suggestions, expertise, information, or photographs to this book. Mention in this regard of any individual or organization does not, of course, imply their acceptance or knowledge of or agreement with any of the theories expressed in this book except those specifically attributed to them.

The author wishes to express his especial appreciation to J. Manson Valentine, Ph.D., Curator Honoris of the Museum of Science of Miami and Research Associate of the Bishop Museum of Honolulu, for his drawings, maps, photographs and interviews, as quoted in the text.

The following names are listed in alphabetical order: Norman Beam, author, lecturer, UFO investigator

José María Bensaúde, President, Navecor Lines, Portugal and the Azores Islands

Valerie Berlitz, author, artist

Boeing Commercial Airplane Company

Hugh Auchincloss Brown, electronic engineer, author

Jean Byrd, President, Isis

Edgar Evans Cayce, electrical engineer, author

Hugh Lynn Cayce, President, Association for Research and Enlightenment

Diane Cleaver, editor, author

Julius Egloff, Jr., oceanographer

Fairchild Industries

Mel Fisher, salvor, diver

Athley Gamber, President, Red Aircraft

Carlos González G., UFO researcher

Professor Charles Hapgood, cartographer, historian, author

Dr. Bruce Heezen, oceanographer, author

Captain Don Henry, shipmaster, diver

Robert Hieronimus, author, artist, President, AUM

J. Silva Júnior, Director "Terra Nostra," Azores Islands

Theodora Kane, educator, artist

Edward E. Kuhnel, attorney: specialist, oceanic law

The Library of Congress

Captain Gene Lore, senior pilot, TWA

Howard Metz, pyramidologist

Albert C. Muller, radiation physicist

National Archives and Records Service

Alan C. Nelson, yachtsman

Thomas O'Herron, U. S. Embassy, Lisbon

Arnold Post, author, oceanographer, diver

Reynolds Metals Company

Iván T. Sanderson, explorer, zoologist, author, founder of SITU

Sabina Sanderson, author, researcher, Director, SITU

Gardner Soule, author, oceanographer

John Wallace Spencer, author, lecturer, UFO and Bermuda Triangle investigator

Jim Thorne, oceanographer, shipmaster, diver, author

Carl Payne Tobey, mathematician, astronomer, astrologer, author

Carolyn Tyson, marine painter

Paul J. Tzimoulis, oceanographer, author, publisher, photographer

United States Air Force

United States Coast Guard

United States Navy

Vijay Verma, Government of India Tourist Office

Charles Wakeley, airplane and helicopter pilot

G. Theon Wright, author, explorer, psychic researcher

Roy H. Wirshing, Lieutenant Commander, USN-Ret., lecturer, author

Robie Yonge, pilot, commentator, UFO investigator

Bibliography

BEFORE MENTION OF SOME OF THE BOOKS REFERRED to in the present work, the author would like to recommend to the reader's attention the *Bermuda Triangle Bibliography* compiled by Larry Kusche and Deborah Blouin, Arizona State University Library, April 1973, which contains numerous references, including books and newspaper and magazine articles, pertaining to the Bermuda Triangle. While hundreds of authors are cited in this bibliography, the most concrete and complete references to the Bermuda Triangle phenomena can be found in the works of Sanderson, Gaddis, and Spencer, listed below, inter alia.

Barker, Ralph, *Great Mysteries of the Air*. London, 1966.

Berlitz, Charles, *Mysteries from Forgotten Worlds*.
            New York, 1972.

The Bible   King James Version.

Blumrich, J., *The Space Ships of Ezekiel*. New
            York, 1973.

Bosworth, A. R., *My Love Affair with the Navy*.
            New York, 1969.

Briggs, Peter, *Men in the Sea*. New York, 1968.

Brown, Hugh Auchincloss, *Cataclysms of the Earth*.
            New York, 1967.

Burgess, Robert F., · *Sinkings, Salvages, and Ship-
            wrecks*. New York, 1970.

Carnac, Pierre, *L'histoire commence à Bimini*.
            Paris, 1973.

Chevalier, Raymond, *L'avion à la découverte du
            passé*. Paris, 1964.

Edwards, Frank, *Stranger Than Science*. New York,
            1959.

————   *Strangest of All*. New York, 1956.

Freuchen, Peter, *Peter Freuchen's Book of the
            Seven Seas*. New York, 1957.

Fuller, John G., *Incident at Exeter*. New York,
            1966.

Gaddis, Vincent, *Invisible Horizons*. Philadelphia,
            1965.

Gaston, Patrice, *Disparitions mystérieuses*. Paris,
            1973.

Godwin, John, *This Baffling World*. New York,
            1968.

Gould, Rupert T., *Enigmas*. New York, 1965.

Keyhoe, Donald E., *Flying Saucer Conspiracy*.
            London, 1955.

Kosok, Paul, *Land, Life and Water in Ancient
            Peru*. New York, 1965.

The Mahabharata, Translated by Protap Chandra Roy. Calcutta, 1889.

The Mahavira

O'Donnell, Elliot, *Strange Sea Mysteries.* London, 1926.

Sagan, Carl, *Intelligent Life in the Universe.* San Francisco, 1966.

Sanderson, Ivan T., *Invisible Residents: A Disquisition upon Certain Matters Maritime, and the Possibility of Intelligent Life Under the Waters of This Earth.* New York, 1970.

——— *Investigating the Unexplained.* Englewood Cliffs, New Jersey, 1972.

Snow, Edward Rowe, *Mysteries and Adventures Along the Atlantic Coast.* 1948.

Soule, Gardner, *Undersea Frontiers.* Chicago, 1968.

——— *Ocean Adventure.* New York, 1964.

——— *Wide Ocean.* Chicago, 1970.

——— *Under the Sea.* New York, 1971.

Spencer, John Wallace, *Limbo of the Lost.* Westfield, Mass., 1969.

Steiger, Brad, *Atlantis Rising.* New York, 1973.

Stewart, Oliver, *Danger in the Air.* New York, 1958.

Stick, David, *Graveyard of the Atlantic.* Chapel Hill, 1952.

Titler, Dale, *Wings of Mystery, Riddles of Aviation History.* New York, 1966.

Tomas, Andrew, *We Are Not the First*. London, 1971.

Tucker, Terry, *Beware the Hurricane!* Bermuda, 1966.

Villiers, Alan, *Wild Ocean*. New York, 1957.

Waters, Frank, *Book of the Hopi*. New York, 1969.

Wilkins, Harold T., *Flying Saucers on the Attack*. New York, 1954.

——— *Strange Mysteries of Time and Space*. New York, 1959.

THE ELECTRIFYING TRUE STORY OF THE MOST DARING MANHUNT OF OUR TIME!

After-math

BY

Ladislas Farago

Bestselling Author of
THE GAME OF THE FOXES and PATTON

The *true* story of Ladislas Farago's courageous and relentless search for the Führer's right-hand-man and confidant, Martin Bormann . . . and how he finally came face-to-face with the most wanted Nazi war criminal of all!

**A REAL-LIFE SAGA OF SUSPENSE
AND INTERNATIONAL INTRIGUE**

"THE STUFF OF WHICH THRILLERS ARE MADE."
Los Angeles Times

25387 / $1.95

THE THUNDERING NOVEL
OF EARLY MAN'S BRUTAL STRUGGLE
TOWARD CIVILIZATION

Irving A. Greenfield's

ATON

The powerful saga of Aton, a man locked in a time of bloody violence and the savage, primitive passions of prehistory.

Irving Greenfield's ATON—a bizarre, shattering, totally unforgettable foray into man's primal past—and the strange life-force that leads man to evolve, to struggle, to survive!

The new novel
by the bestselling author of
A PLAY OF DARKNESS
and
THE ANCIENT OF DAYS.